SIMPLIFY YOUR

Workday

A **Reader's Digest Simpler Life**™ Book

Designed, edited, and produced by Weldon Owen

THE READER'S DIGEST ASSOCIATION, INC.

Group Editorial Director, Cooking/Home/Consumer Books Carol Guasti

Group Design Director, Cooking/Home/Consumer Books Joan Mazzeo

Project Editor Candace Conard

Project Art Director Jane Wilson

WELDON OWEN INC.

President John Owen

Publisher Roger S. Shaw

Series Editor Janet Goldenberg

Contributing Editors Mandy Erickson, Bonnie Monte

Copy Editors Lisa R. Bornstein, Gail Nelson

Art Director Elizabeth Marken

Design Consultant Emma Forge

Production Designer Brynn Breuner

Design Assistant William Erik Evans

Icon Illustrator Matt Graif

Production Director Stephanie Sherman

Production Manager Jen Dalton

Project Photographers Chris Shorten, Brian Pierce

Photo Stylist JoAnn Masaoka Van Atta

Photo Editor Melinda Lawson

A Reader's Digest/Weldon Owen Publication

Printed in China

*A note on weights and measures: Metric equivalences given for
U.S. weights and measures are approximate. Actual equivalences may vary.*

SIMPLIFY YOUR
Workday

BARBARA HEMPHILL & PAMELA QUINN GIBBARD

Illustrations by TRAVIS FOSTER

Reader's Digest

The Reader's Digest Association, Inc.
Pleasantville, New York/Montreal

CONTENTS

You can master the challenges of your workday
by learning how to balance its demands.

LESS STRESS, MORE SUCCESS

———✳———

D_o you go to work each morning dreading the stress-filled day ahead—a high-wire act fraught with endless meetings, a constantly jangling phone, difficult coworkers, and technology that makes your job harder rather than easier? Is your desk a tower of paperwork that piles up faster than you can clear it away? Back at home, do you struggle with chores and child care routines that leave you exhausted the next day? If so, you've probably thought there has to be a better way. Well, there is—and this book will help you discover it.

Simplify Your Workday outlines the most effective timesaving techniques and stress-reducing strategies we've discovered in our 20 years as professional organizers—one of us with a blended family of five children, the other a single parent. Much of the material we present focuses on work in an office setting, but the basic principles apply to other work situations as well. Whether your workplace is a cubicle, a sales floor, or your spare bedroom, you'll find advice here that can help make each day run more smoothly.

The journey begins with learning to manage your time more effectively. We'll show you how to get a handle on routine tasks such as attending meetings, managing projects, and tackling your in box, as well as special challenges—making the most of computer software, giving presentations, dealing with problem coworkers, traveling, and staying in touch with colleagues and customers. Organizing your personal routine will make it easier to get to work on time and make your evenings and weekends more relaxing.

You'll also find powerful techniques for getting a grip on paperwork. We'll show you how to decide what to keep, where to keep it, and how to find it when you need it— whether it's in your filing cabinet or on your computer.

Some changes you can make are simple ones that will improve things right away. Others may take a little longer, but this book will guide you through the process. We've provided easy-to-use checklists and identified a variety of resources to help you simplify your workday from beginning to end.

Accept the reality that changing your behavior takes time, and don't worry about how long—just get started! It's important to remember that no method or system will work every time in every situation, so refine as you go along. And when you make a mistake, forgive yourself and move on. Simplifying is about progress—not perfectionism.

Enjoy your journey!

Barbara Hemphill

Pamela Quinn Gibbard

You'll be flying through your workday once
you master a few simple techniques.

SIMPLE SYMBOLS

———— ✳ ————

IN EACH CHAPTER OF THIS BOOK you'll find nuggets of advice for easing every part of your workday—from getting out of the house in the morning to wrapping up the last to-do item at night. These quick tips will help you get the job done more efficiently and with less stress, whatever your assignment or goal. Look for boxes marked with symbols in the following helpful categories:

 Labor Savers help you ease your workload whenever it seems there's just too much to be done. Refer to these boxes to find out how to get more done with less effort so you'll feel more relaxed at the end of a long, hard day.

 Time Savers explain how to shave minutes or even hours from your day without compromising the quality of your work. Follow these tips to make the best use of each minute so you can succeed at your work and still have time for a life.

 Bright Ideas offer tips to help solve problems in the workplace, enhance your work environment, organize your office, and inspire you to reach your goals. These ideas—like many important concepts—are surprisingly easy to implement.

 Simply Safer suggestions offer strategies to reduce your risks on the job. They provide advice on safeguarding your health and protecting yourself against situations that may put you in jeopardy at work. Just one of these simple tips could help you avoid pain or lost workdays. It could even save your job.

 Stress Busters provide simple, surefire methods to overcome procrastination, avoid overload, and get help from coworkers and friends. These tips will help you relieve the pressures of the job so you can enjoy your work as well as excel at it.

 Cost Cutters help you make the most of your company's dollar—and your own money— by conserving your resources and spending them wisely. Use these tips to save hard-earned cash in your home-based business activities as well.

 Rules of Thumb will help you function more effectively with proven principles such as what portion of the time to devote to listening versus talking at a meeting, and how to decide on the computer equipment that's best for your needs.

 Don't Forget tips offer handy pointers that may appear obvious but that are easy to forget during the hustle and bustle of your workday. Reaching your goals and enjoying yourself at work are your first priorities, so refer to these boxes to help keep yourself on track and in the right frame of mind.

MAXIMIZING
your Day

1 Break down long-term projects into smaller **tasks** that you can accomplish day by day. **2** Make timely **decisions** in order to keep your projects on track and your desk free of clutter. **3** Fight procrastination by making a **start,** even if it's just writing a to-do list. **4** Use a printed or electronic **calendar,** not your memory, to stay on top of your schedule. **5** Maintain both master and daily **to-do lists** to keep your projects moving. **6** Carve out large **blocks of time** by minimizing interruptions. If you need to, hang a "Busy" sign on the back of your chair. **7** Run more effective **meetings** by aiming for decisions rather than just discussions. **8** Manage those stacks of **reading materials:** Recycle or trash the articles and publications that aren't essential. **9** Whenever it's appropriate, **delegate** tasks to others. Junior staff members will welcome the chance to learn from more challenging assignments. **10** Don't forget to **take breaks**—they will clear your head and help you work more efficiently. ●

MANAGING
YOUR TIME

GETTING IT ALL DONE
WITHOUT GOING CRAZY

＊──────＊──────＊

The simple truth about time is that we are all stuck with the same 60-minute hour, 24-hour day, and 7-day week. It's how you use that time that determines what you can accomplish in an hour, a day, a week, a career, or a lifetime. More important, your use of time determines your level of satisfaction in life. True fulfillment comes not merely from keeping busy, but from using your time in a meaningful way.

At work, however, it's far too easy to fall into the trap of busying yourself with the small details of the day. Managing your workday will be easier if you focus on the big picture first. Then you can balance your priorities, make better decisions, and carry out those decisions with confidence. There are many things you cannot control, but using some basic time-management strategies will simplify your workday and increase your fundamental satisfaction as well.

SETTING PRIORITIES

---※---

Work is landing on your desk from every direction, the deadline for presentation materials is tomorrow, and you've just been asked to represent the department at a big meeting in two hours.

In today's busy world, priorities change constantly, so flexibility is essential. But allowing yourself to be pushed and pulled by each new demand as it arises is clearly counterproductive. Instead of working *harder,* focus on working *smarter*—make sure that you're doing the right thing at the right time, and ask yourself whether you should be doing it at all.

FIRST THINGS FIRST

Although it may seem frivolous when you are struggling to keep up with the day's tasks, the first place to look when managing your time is at the big picture. Ask yourself what you like and dislike about your job. Are you in the right career? With the right company? Doing the right job?

Organizational tips and techniques won't be worth much in the long run if the job you're doing is not right for you.

Everyone has bad days at work, but if you find you're not enjoying yourself most of the time, some fundamental changes may be in order. If you work for a law firm and you love the mental challenge, but your company seems to be the prototype for bad-lawyer jokes, you might want to consider another firm. On the other hand, if you love the workplace but feel bored and underused, it may be time to talk to your supervisor about new opportunities.

Brainstorming with coworkers *can help you set priorities and identify ways to work smarter rather than harder.*

Even if you consider it a hypothetical exercise, ask yourself what is in your heart of hearts. Do you want to make junior partner? Be a successful songwriter? Perhaps you just want to get out of debt or make enough money to send your children to private school. If you don't know what's truly important to you at this stage of your life, then it's worth thinking about—and it's absolutely crucial if you want to become an efficient time manager.

What kind of job change might support your dream? If you need a degree to help achieve it, find out if your employer will pay for continuing education. Do you need more experience? Perhaps local volunteer programs could use your help and enable you to cultivate new skills.

Taking small steps toward your goal will improve your morale significantly—and make your workday more rewarding.

The process of identifying your goals may take a while, so start now. Pay particular attention to the times when you feel good at work. What tasks are you performing? Are you working alone or with others? What kinds of people stimulate you? The more you learn about yourself, the easier it will be to find a job you truly enjoy.

Circumstances may make it impossible for you to change course suddenly and pursue exactly the kind of career that you want. But taking small steps leading you in that direction will improve your morale significantly—and make your workday

Accentuate the Positive

Measuring yourself by what you have accomplished—instead of by what you haven't—can help motivate you to further action. Instead of saying, "I still have to sell 10 more units to meet my quota," say, "I've already sold more than last year, and I'm halfway to this year's goal."

more rewarding. Start off by identifying a specific goal, such as increasing your salary by 20 percent, getting a board position in your professional association, or earning a teaching credential. Then identify some specific actions you'll need to take to attain that goal. Studies show that only 2 percent of the population have identified concrete goals for themselves. Write yours down and look at them daily. Ask yourself: What can I do today to be one step closer to my dream?

DAY-TO-DAY DECISIONS
Once you've established a path to your ultimate career goal, it's time to focus on the smaller tasks—because regardless of where you want to end up, the success of your journey depends on the decisions you make day by day. But deciding what to do each day and each hour is not an easy task—especially in today's fast-paced work environments. When you're faced

If in Doubt, Decide

Indecision is nearly always the worst mistake you can make. When tempted to postpone a decision, ask yourself: What will I know tomorrow that I don't know today? If the answer is nothing, just make the best decision you can and move ahead. In many cases, you will be able to adjust your course as you get more information.

with an onslaught of ever-changing, late-breaking information, it's sometimes hard to weigh the data and make a decision in a timely manner. There are other reasons, too, why you may put off making important decisions. You may think:

◆ I DON'T WANT TO MAKE A MISTAKE.

◆ I DON'T KNOW ENOUGH ABOUT THE SUBJECT.

◆ I DON'T WANT TO TAKE THE RESPONSIBILITY.

◆ I'M AFRAID IT WON'T BE PERFECT.

Some of these reasons may be appropriate in certain situations—such as when it's imperative to prevent mistakes, determine that the decision is not your responsibility, or find out whether you truly need more information. But while taking more time may reveal a better solution to a problem, the odds are against it. What's more, if you repeatedly put off making decisions, you're virtually guaranteed to face a continuous backlog of projects needing

completion, frustrated colleagues or customers, and a cluttered work environment. And consider this: Not making a decision is in itself a decision—one whose outcome may not be what you want.

A PLAN OF ATTACK

This six-step decision-making plan can help you attack any problem or project:

Step one. State the question clearly. This may sound obvious, but it's a step many people omit. It's important to know exactly what the goals and issues are, especially when other people in the company may have conflicting agendas. Whether you send an e-mail or nail down the issues at a meeting, make sure that everyone who needs to know understands the goal.

Step two. Gather relevant information. Do your homework to find out the necessary background information. This could include talking with people inside and outside the company, examining written data, or consulting with experts in the field. But don't get so bogged down in research that it becomes an end in itself.

Step three. Evaluate all possible solutions. In most cases, there will be several reasonable alternatives, each with its own pros and cons. Consider the implications of each approach by weighing the relative merits in whatever way is most appropriate: Run what-if scenarios in a spreadsheet program or meet with your colleagues to discuss the potential strengths and drawbacks of each possible alternative.

Step four. Identify ways to reduce the risk of failure. Play devil's advocate and consider the ways your plan could derail.

For example, a key staffer could leave at a critical moment; a project could prove more complex and costly than anticipated; a devastating piece of news could arrive at the last minute. It's a very rare situation in which *everything* goes wrong, but it's also a rare case in which everything goes right. To the extent that you can, try to anticipate any potential roadblocks and devise effective work-arounds in advance.

Step five. Make a decision based on the best projections available. Information gathering is at best an imperfect art, and the future is unpredictable: These are facts that all decision makers must face. All you can do is make the best decision you can, based on the information that you have at the time. If circumstances change along the way, you can often make adjustments.

Step six. Begin implementing the decision. Start putting your plan into action, if only by making entries on a calendar.

If necessary, explain to your supervisor or colleagues how the new plan will make work go more smoothly or increase

Evaluate each option *before making a decision—but don't delay too long. It's better to move forward than to remain in limbo.*

customer satisfaction. Writing down a game plan or articulating it to others is the first step toward making it happen.

GETTING STARTED

The best decision in the world is useless if it isn't followed by action. The fact is, we all procrastinate at times. Many people quickly finish those things in which they excel and delay the jobs in which they feel less competent. You may speed through those statistical reports but find yourself still working away on tomorrow morning's oral presentation at midnight—or even the next morning. Sometimes we procrastinate in the hope that a task will go away. Once in a while that method works—somebody else eventually takes care of it!

At other times the underlying cause of the procrastination is more complex—motivated perhaps by fear of failure or

Forced Labor

If a deadline is near and you still can't get yourself to start on a project, try working in a secluded location with no distractions. Tell yourself you can't leave until you finish. An empty conference room, an unused cubicle, the office of a colleague who's out of town—all are good places to sequester yourself so you can get down to work.

Build in a deadline. Set realistic milestones and deadlines for projects that you never seem to get around to, and communicate those goals to someone else to keep yourself accountable. You'll have that report out of your hair if you tell your boss you will get it done by Monday.

Find a simpler alternative. If you've been putting off writing a letter, maybe a phone call would be an easier solution. Or how about sending a quick e-mail?

Tackle your insecurities. If you delay preparing for an oral presentation because you're afraid of public speaking, role-play with a friend until you feel comfortable.

Break down large tasks. A huge project tends to be overwhelming; short, easy tasks are more appealing and can provide quick gratification. Instead of trying to bang out an entire sales report, why not set a goal of just writing an outline? The simple act of beginning often can give you enough momentum to continue.

even by fear of success. For some people, procrastination creates last-minute pressure, which they find motivating. But if your procrastination consistently causes you to do less-than-stellar work, then it's time for you to find a new approach.

When faced with a job you've been avoiding, perhaps the first question to ask yourself is, What is the worst thing that would happen if I didn't do this? If you

Reward yourself. Be good to yourself at each step, not just at completion. Perks along the way can keep you motivated.

Overcome procrastination by setting realistic deadlines and communicating them to someone else to keep yourself accountable.

can live with the results, cross the task off your list. If it must be done, however, here are some strategies that can help:

Consider delegating. This doesn't mean passing the buck. Someone on your staff who excels in an area in which you're weak might be happy to take on the challenge. Perhaps your department's budget will let you hire someone to handle the task.

Stay in touch. Make your progress public, especially to people affected by your decisions. Also, establish a regular time when you and your boss can meet, identify priorities, and reassess them if it's necessary. Knowing that your colleagues are aware of your progress and that your boss is going to provide timely feedback will help you implement decisions more confidently.

STAYING ON TRACK

❋

SELECTING EXACTLY THE RIGHT TIME-MANAGEMENT TOOLS—APPOINTMENT BOOKS, WALL CALENDARS, LOOSE-LEAF PLANNING SYSTEMS, OR SCHEDULING SOFTWARE—IS VITAL TO KEEPING YOUR WORKDAY RUNNING SMOOTHLY.

Happily, the choices are nearly endless. In fact, many systems are so loaded with features that you'll need a one- or two-day course just to figure out how to use them. Why not keep it simple? Three basic tools will do the job: a calendar or planner, a master to-do list, and a daily to-do list.

CHOOSING A CALENDAR

How do you remember when your next project meeting is? Or your appointment with human resources? Or the dentist visit (which you'd rather forget)? If you rely on your memory, you're going to slip up. You need a place to record everything.

There are countless options for calendars, in both paper and electronic form. You can buy many of them at your local office-supply stores, while others are sold only through mail order. It's a sign of these busy times that stores specializing in time-management products are starting to open in malls across North America. Not only can you get basic calendars and planners in all sizes and shapes, but you'll also find them paired with purses, briefcases, calculators, and other workday accessories.

It's easy to fall into the trap of believing that lots of snazzy sections, specialized pages, and accessories will *really* get you organized, but months later you may still not have figured out exactly how to use them (or even whether you need them).

Selecting a calendar is very much a matter of taste, and with all the options available, you may feel overwhelmed.

Wrestling with deadlines is easier if you have the right tools.

GETTING THROUGH THE DAY'S AGENDA
CAN BE A CHALLENGE. THESE TOOLS HELP
YOU DO IT ALL IN TIMELY FASHION.

Appointment book

The backbone of any scheduling effort, this book is your lifeline when you're juggling many tasks and responsibilities. Use it to schedule appointments as well as highlight the action items from your master to-do list.

Electronic planner

A pocket-size planner is perfect for tracking time and responsibilities wherever you are. You can set it to beep when it's time for the next item in your daily schedule.

Magnetic note board

Keep the day's to-do list clearly in view: Post important notes to yourself on this magnetic board or write them in bold letters on the sheets of paper attached.

Clock and hourglass

Nothing is better than these old-fashioned tools for reminding you and your visitors that time is precious. Keep yours in full view. An hourglass can be purely decorative or it can serve a useful function: If you're chairing a meeting, carry one with you and (depending on how much sand it contains) use it to set a time limit on the discussion of agenda items or on the meeting as a whole.

The choice becomes even more complex when you need to share calendar information with other people. Some companies, for instance, require everyone to use an on-line calendar to make scheduling meetings and events easy. If you don't like that format, you may choose to keep a personal calendar in addition to the company's. If your professional life extends into evenings and weekends with client dinners and other social events, combining your personal and professional life on one calendar may prove helpful, if not essential.

The best time to buy (and try) a calendar is usually near the beginning of the year, when they are readily available. The more sophisticated systems, however, let you start with any month of the year. You'll be using your calendar daily, so don't feel embarrassed if one of your primary concerns is how it looks or feels: That's not as superficial as it sounds.

With loose-leaf systems, you always have the option of combining elements you like from different systems to create a personalized arrangement that suits your needs. If even the basic system is too complex, it may still be useful. You can keep only those sections you know you'll use and lighten your load by removing everything else. You can always add sections back if you find that you need them later.

A MASTER TO-DO LIST

Unless you're aware of all the things that you need to do in a given day or week, it is virtually impossible for you to figure out what to do first or last. And you shouldn't rely on your memory to hold and update a constantly changing number of tasks. One simple solution is to keep a running master to-do list. This list is the key to effective time management—it provides the fundamental data from which all of your workday planning, scheduling, and prioritizing will emerge.

Get out a blank sheet of paper (or fire up your word processor) and write down everything you can think of that you need to get done. Keep the list handy during the course of the day so you can add tasks as

Life isn't always about squeezing more activities onto the head of a pin. Reaching your goals depends on how well you prioritize.

you think of them. Don't worry if you need more than a page. The object is to engage in a mind dump that gets everything out of your head and onto the paper. Once you've written down everything you can think of, go back and break large projects into smaller chunks or stages.

As you look for ways to simplify, you should consider not only how to organize your work but also what you can eliminate. Life isn't always about squeezing more activities onto the head of a pin. The "do more, do it faster" approach of the 1980's and 1990's is giving way to a time of more sensibility and balance. Reaching your goals depends on how well you prioritize, not on how many tasks you complete.

As you finish items on your list, cross them off (it's much more fun than making a check mark). Keep adding new items as

they come up. Don't bother to recopy or transfer items to a new list—just keep adding and crossing off. A nifty place to keep your master to-do list is in your planner, so it's always handy as you update it and add or cross off items.

A DAILY TO-DO LIST

As you plan the coming day before leaving the office or starting work in the morning, move the appropriate items from the master to-do list to a daily to-do list. Before you move each item, ask yourself: Should this task be done now, and who's the best person to do it—me or someone else? If the answer is someone else, then ask: Who should that individual be?

Many calendars and planners are formatted with daily to-do sections ready to use. However, if you're using a calendar without such a section, you can simply put a sticky note on today's calendar page.

Calendar Basics

It's not the price tag that determines the value of a calendar, but rather what it's worth to you. Figure out what your needs are (a calendar that displays each month on one page, for example, or a planner that you can customize) and use the simplest tool that meets those needs. Don't waste your money on any unnecessary bells and whistles.

Your 15 Most Important Minutes

At the end of each day—when projects are left hanging as you pack up for home—take 15 minutes to list the most important things to do the next day: calls to return, meetings to attend, projects to complete. This will keep details from falling through the cracks and make the next day more productive.

In fact, those who prefer visual reminders can cover a clipboard with a sticky note for each task to do that day, and move the notes around for easy, instant reassessment of priorities. You can peel off sticky notes and toss them in the trash as you accomplish each task—a satisfying act—and allow the notes for as-yet-uncompleted tasks to stick around until tomorrow.

Some time-management strategists encourage people to identify priorities using the letters *A, B,* and *C* to designate the importance of each task: A tasks are the highest-priority, must-do items (such as submitting a bid before a deadline); B tasks are should-do items (such as prospecting for new clients); and C tasks are could-do items (such as organizing your desk drawers). Another way to do this type of prioritizing is to list all the items on a page, then highlight each item in a color that indicates its priority. You can buy highlighter pens in sets of four bold

shades—use three to indicate the A, B, and C priorities, and the other color for want-to-do tasks (such as shopping for clothes during your lunch hour), which may not further your professional aims but are appealing nevertheless. Getting these tasks out of your brain and onto paper may help you make wise choices, and you can always use these want-to-dos as rewards for the milestones or goals you have reached.

Whatever approach you use, however, it's critical to identify the one or two most important tasks to do each day. In fact, when you start to feel overwhelmed with your workload, take a minute to ask yourself: What is the *most important* thing I could do with my time right now? Note that there's a difference between tasks that need doing right away, such as getting someone's signature before he or she goes into a meeting, and tasks that are important to finish to keep yourself on track toward a goal. Dispose of the urgent tasks as quickly as you can so you can concentrate on what's really important.

PROJECT PLANNING

Coordinating a complex project with a deadline can be a challenge, whether it's producing a sales report for your business or overseeing the move of your entire office to a new location. No matter what size your project, the first step is to specify the desired outcome and the deadline. Next, list all the major tasks that you must complete before you can reach your goal. For example, if you're compiling the sales report, you'll likely need the latest statistics before you can write up a summary

and projection. You'll also have to get the spreadsheet and word-processing files that are associated with those statistics before you or a graphic artist can lay out the document on a computer. And you'll need bids from a duplicating service before you can schedule printing and binding.

Request the necessary information right away, give deadlines, and make sure everyone is able to meet them. Let team members know that if they miss deadlines, the entire project could fall off track. If there's only one person who can supply you with a crucial piece of information, you'll want to make sure that he or she can work this task into his or her schedule. Also, make sure to spread the work out evenly so one individual doesn't become overloaded and create a bottleneck.

To assist you in keeping on top of all the moving parts, draw up a flowchart showing which tasks need to be done and the dates when those tasks need to be completed. Project planning software can

Gain a sense *of accomplishment by identifying the most important tasks to complete each day and updating colleagues on your progress.*

help you create flowcharts and record the progress of the project. For a project planning template, see page 132.

Parkinson's Law

British historian C. Northcote Parkinson observed that work expands to fill the time available for it. That is, if there's room in a schedule, people will find things to do that may not really be necessary. Thus, it's often better to leave barely enough time to finish up a project than it is to provide more than enough time.

Taking Charge of Your Day

————— ✳ —————

How often have you gone to work convinced that today would be the day you'd catch up—only to find that the hours mysteriously slipped away and that you accomplished next to nothing?

Minimizing the interruptions, managing meetings, delegating tasks, and surviving the information deluge are ongoing concerns critical to your business success and your personal well-being.

The week's demands can be intense, but with effective time management you can get the job done and save your weekends to renew, rejuvenate, and bring some balance back into your life.

If your day is filled with a barrage of phone calls and coworkers popping in and out of your office, you may not realize just how much time this gobbles up. Experts

estimate that after each interruption, it takes 10 to 15 minutes for anyone to get back on track. If you add up those calls and visits throughout your day, you'll see how much damage interruptions can do to your already tight schedule.

QUIET, PLEASE

To maximize your day, you need to minimize interruptions that steal your attention from the task at hand. First, determine their sources. Are you getting calls that you shouldn't be fielding? Let the person at the front desk know where to direct

Letting coworkers know you're temporarily off-limits
gives you the time to finish important tasks.

SIMPLE SOLUTIONS

DEALING WITH OVERLOAD

NO MATTER HOW WELL YOU PLAN your schedule, sometimes it seems as if everything you're working on is due on the same day. When the work starts to pile up, the smartest—and simplest—thing to do is to find ways to ease the load.

Simple Trade work with colleagues. If you can hand off some of your projects, see if less-busy coworkers are willing to ease your load. You can help them out when your workload has lightened up.

Simpler Hire a temporary worker or contract the work out. You may be able to justify the expense to your boss if you show that getting everything done promptly will save the company money.

Simplest Put a hold on the tasks that aren't essential or see if you can push back a deadline. If you investigate, you may find that the client won't be able to respond to your bid until next week anyway.

them. Does small talk with colleagues hamper your progress? Learn to curtail conversations when they turn from business exchanges to social patter—or tell people who stop by that you have only a minute to chat. Even rearranging your work space can help: Move your desk so that you aren't visible to everyone who walks down the hall. People are less likely to engage you in casual talk if they can't make eye contact with you.

You can also try another valuable technique for improving time management: Set aside a block of time each day (even an hour will help) during which no one can interrupt you. Ask your coworkers to cooperate with the plan and promise them the same consideration. If possible, pick your peak energy time. Inform your boss about the plan, explaining the specific benefits you expect to gain—indicate projects or reports that you are working on.

Simply shut your door at the designated time, route your calls to voice mail or have someone else answer your phone, then roll up your sleeves. If you don't have the luxury of an office with a door, move to another location or put a "Please do not disturb" sign on the back of your chair. You'll be amazed (and your boss will be pleased) at what you can accomplish during this period. Make sure you use this valuable time to tackle the project with the highest priority—not to finish some simple task that you could work on just as effectively at another time.

Remember to open your office door or to remove your "Do not disturb" sign when the time is up, and promptly return those calls. Isolation, even when it's for a worthy cause, can negatively affect vital communications if it's abused.

On the other hand, your time-out strategy may encourage other people to do the same, improving overall productivity in the office. You might even consider suggesting a daily no-interruptions hour for your whole department—a time when everyone on staff can work without the

If it's truly necessary that you attend and give input at a meeting, ask if you can sit in on just those agenda items that are relevant to you.

intrusion of phone calls or meetings. This hour will provide an astonishing opportunity for focus and concentration, while leaving the majority of the day available for collaboration and communication.

A well-run meeting *gives everyone a chance to voice opinions and reach consensus without wasting time on small talk. Push for a decision rather than more discussion.*

Finally, if you need a long stretch of undiluted time to complete your project, work in another space for several hours. An on-site empty office or conference room will do the trick. But wherever you go, be certain that you let at least one person know where to find you.

MANAGING MEETINGS

Do you seem to spend more time attending meetings than you do sitting at a desk? Meetings are costly to a business because they tie up so many people at once. If you can find ways to cut unnecessary meetings from your workday, you'll not only be helping the company's bottom line, you'll also be freeing up time for yourself.

For every meeting you're expected to attend, assess whether there's a more efficient way to accomplish the same thing. Consider sending out an announcement or a request for information via memo or e-mail. In some situations, a telephone conference call or videoconferencing can achieve the same goals while saving you significant time and travel expenses.

Just as it's crucial to plan your day, it's important to plan your meetings. A well-thought-out agenda makes an amazing difference in the quality and value of any meeting, whether it lasts 15 minutes or three days. If you are chairing the meeting, there are a number of techniques that can streamline your job:

Circulate your agenda ahead of time. Include the topics that you plan to cover, with a request (as well as a deadline) for giving feedback prior to the meeting. Give a time frame for discussing each topic.

Whenever possible, assign individuals to chair specific topics. That way, people will show up for the meeting well prepared.

Invite only those who need to attend. Include everyone with responsibility for the items to be discussed. Not only will the meeting go faster with fewer people there, but those not required to attend can get on with other tasks.

Keep to your agenda. If tangential topics arise, note them for inclusion in the next meeting's agenda rather than letting them take up time in the current meeting. If a topic goes over the time budgeted, table it for the next meeting.

Always begin your meeting right on time. Waiting 5 or 10 minutes to start sends the message that it's acceptable to be tardy. And don't recap when latecomers arrive—simply let people slip into the room.

Push for decisions. Discussing issues without coming to decisions wastes an astonishing amount of valuable time. Try not to let a meeting come to an end without making some kind of decision.

Schedule wisely. Whenever it's possible, schedule meetings to leave big blocks of the day intact. If a series of meetings are necessary, group them together in either the morning or afternoon. Scheduling one meeting right after another will encourage you to finish the first one on time.

Take stock. When the meeting is over, ask yourself if there's anything you could have done to make it better. If the answer is yes, make sure you do that next time.

For meetings that you're not leading, evaluate carefully whether your presence is really necessary. If you're not convinced

Pruning Paper

If you're a department head, circulate a list of all publications the department orders and ask staff members to check off those they have read in the past year. Cancel the subscriptions that no one is reading. Magazines and newspapers often get buried on people's desks; create a central library where everyone can access materials.

that it's worth your time, ask your supervisor if you can skip it. Maybe you can read the minutes, if they're available. If it's truly necessary that you attend a meeting, ask if you can attend for just those agenda items that are relevant to you.

TAMING YOUR READING

You're not alone if masses of unread material threaten to take over your work space, making you feel guilty every day they go untouched. (Unfortunately, the paperless office promised a decade ago still has not arrived.) It's no accident that the business world today abounds with newsletters that condense critical information.

Face it—no matter how many speed-reading courses you take, you will never be able to read everything you want to, or think you ought to. And when you do get to something, it's difficult to remember what you've read when you're overwhelmed with information. Some ways to simplify:

Taking a short break now and then
helps you focus better on the job.

Perform triage. Determine what information sources are absolutely vital to your field and eliminate the less valuable ones. Set aside one or two hours per week for the things you really must read.

File for later. Rather than trying to keep everything that's relevant to your job, file specific articles to read when projects arise. (For filing tips, see pages 76–79.)

Rely on the Internet. Go online to read newspapers and find the latest and greatest information whenever you need it.

Read on the run. Keep reading material in a folder you can carry in your briefcase to skim during downtime, when you're waiting for a meeting to start, for a cab to arrive, or for the dentist to call your name.

Save just the good parts. Eliminate those stacks of bulky magazines by clipping out

or photocopying useful articles. File the articles or carry them with you, and trash or recycle the rest of the magazine.

DELEGATE, DELEGATE

Your desk is covered with projects waiting to be done. Your boss just asked again about the Ramirez proposal, and you have yet to return three phone calls on priority projects. If this sounds familiar, you may be trying to do too much—and you could benefit from judicious delegation. No, you say. You've tried, and it's always a disaster.

It's often hard to let go of work for which you are responsible and trust that others will do it up to your standards—and on time. It also may be difficult for you to give up the notion that you are indispensable to the rest of the office.

If you think that it takes less time to do it yourself than to train someone else, think again. Although in the short run it does take less time for you to do the job, for recurring tasks you will reap the investment in initial training many times over.

Not only does delegation give you the freedom to pursue other assignments, it also helps in building independence and

your head. Bag your lunch and go sit on a bench in the fresh air. Run some errands or work out at a nearby gym.

There are bound to be days when you can't get out of the office. If you must eat at your desk, at least set your work aside during that period to give your brain some downtime. Escaping for a few minutes—if only mentally—can make a big difference.

If you think delegating work is too time consuming, think again. For recurring tasks, you'll reap the investment in training many times over.

self-reliance in coworkers. Delegation at its best should be more than dumping grunt work on subordinates. Handing off jobs that no one else wants doesn't encourage growth, it just creates resentment. Think of delegation as a form of in-house training.

The real key to successful delegating is trust. What's important is not how that person does the job, but the outcome. His or her style may differ considerably from yours, but the results may be equally successful, and sometimes even superior.

A BREAK A DAY

No matter how hectic your day, it's vital to pause for a breather now and then. Plugging away for too many hours without a rest will cause your productivity to flag. Even a short respite can provide a needed boost. Sit back, close your eyes, and do some deep breathing. Or walk around the block. You'll be recharged for the job at hand and may even find you have a fresh approach to a tough problem.

If you are able to leave the office at lunchtime, the change of scenery can clear

Taking a break can be as simple as shifting gears for a while. For example, if you're trying to write a report and words are failing you, try returning a few important calls or updating your to-do list—the sense of accomplishment you gain from one task can energize you to complete another. Be careful, though. There's a fine line between creative digression and procrastination.

Time for Friends

Schedule a fun lunch once a week with an old friend or acquaintance who works for another company. Not only does it help you take a break from coworkers, but your lunch date brings fresh ideas to the table. He or she might suggest a new approach to an old problem or might know a consultant who could contribute to a project.

BREEZING through your **Day**

—✳—

1 **Assess** your daily routine for elements that add stress for you and your family. **2** Get a good night's **sleep.** It'll give you the energy to complete your tasks the next day. **3** Organize clothes and belongings the night before for a quick **departure.** **4** Start the day with a healthful **breakfast,** but if you prefer to head out the door, pack a simple meal to go. **5** Have children help get themselves ready by **organizing** homework and clothes before they go to bed. **6** Make **lunch hour** a time to rejuvenate, not another source of stress in your life. **7** Combine **errands** to save time and minimize hassle. Purchase everything on your list in one shopping area. **8** Remember to take some **downtime** on weekday evenings. You've earned it! **9** Gather the family and delegate **chores** to everyone. Children of all ages will learn responsibility, and you and your spouse will get a break. **10** Make sure you build **relaxation** into your weekend by taking time out for yourself. ●

Streamlining your Routine

AVOIDING HASSLES
ON THE HOME FRONT

✳ ——— ✳ ——— ✳

Your success and sanity on the job are directly related to how things go before and after work. If your clothes look tired and wrinkled because they've been mashed together in the closet, if you're irritable because you've skipped breakfast, if you're running late because the kids missed the bus and you had to drive them to school, you won't be in a position to give the job your best. Likewise, a miserable day at the office can have a harmful effect on the way you feel at home.

Finding ways to streamline your prework and postwork routine can give you a major jump on removing stress from your day. Where should you start? First, make a list with two columns headed "What's working" and "What's not." Analyze your morning and evening routines and fill out the list honestly. Then concentrate on attacking the trouble spots, using the strategies on the following pages.

Starting the Day

---- ✳ ----

Getting off to work in the morning can rate high on the stress meter. Many of us have a host of responsibilities to accomplish— rouse and feed sleepy children, make lunches, find the keys.

The list of tasks may seem unending some mornings, but it need not be so difficult. With some prior planning and improved organizational skills, your mornings can be far less hectic, if not downright relaxed.

You'll cruise through the mornings with a brighter outlook when you've had a full night of sleep. Although cutting into your snooze time may seem like the easiest way to carve out more hours in the day, it's not a good idea. Continually leaving yourself short on sleep inevitably causes bigger problems, such as accidents and illnesses. Sleep-deprived workers are also less productive. They don't have the concentration to focus on their tasks or the patience to handle stressful situations. People who have had plenty of sleep have more energy.

If you often wake up in a daze because you haven't managed to sleep through the night, try to isolate the cause or causes. If indigestion is the culprit, be sure to eat long enough before bedtime so that inner rumblings won't keep you up. Too much caffeine is another hazard: Remember that those lattes, iced teas, and cola beverages add up, and that foods such as chocolate also have their share of this stimulant.

You'll be putting your best foot forward each day once you've mastered the morning routine.

While exercise during the day can prepare you for a better night's sleep, strenuous activity too close to bedtime can rev you up and keep you wide awake. Try to move your exercise regimen to the morning and save the evening for relaxation.

Some medications and medical conditions can play havoc with your slumber. If insomnia remains a persistent problem for you, check with your doctor.

A full night of sleep is a must for children as well. They're cranky and difficult when they're tired, making your morning more stressful. Be firm about bedtime on school nights. If you find that your kids still have trouble getting up, move their bedtime back five minutes each night until they wake early enough to enable everyone to get out of the house on time.

THE RIGHT CLOTHES

Even if you've managed to beat the alarm clock, you might still miss the train if you lose time searching for something to wear. It doesn't help to wake up early if you stand there bleary-eyed, looking at your

The 20/80 Wardrobe Rule

If you're like most people, you probably wear 20 percent of your wardrobe 80 percent of the time. You may dread deciding what to wear, or you may just slip into comfortable habits. But those seldom-worn clothes take up room. Eliminate those you don't wear and save the space.

Yet another alternative is to arrange your clothes by color. If the blues are with blues, and the browns are with browns, it will take you just a minute in the morning to mix or match efficiently. You may even end up seeing more combinations than you ever dreamed you had.

Create a place for clothing items that need repair or dry cleaning, and designate a time to deal with them. Store clothes that

Set aside time one weekend to reorganize your wardrobe. Put like items together—pants, skirts, dresses, jackets, shirts, slacks.

clothes, rejecting one outfit after another: A button is missing. There's a spot on the lapel. The only shoes that work with this suit are nowhere to be found.

Set aside time one weekend to reorganize your wardrobe. Put together items such as pants, skirts, dresses, jackets, shirts, slacks. Or try separating your clothes into categories: formal, workday, and casual.

you rarely wear or that are out-of-season in the basement or attic, and give away any items that you haven't worn for a year.

Organize your accessories as well. You might want to purchase an organizer box to use inside a dresser drawer; or hang hats, ties, necklaces, and belts on a closet door. A wall-mounted expanding mug rack can quickly provide a dozen pegs on which to hang your accessories. If you still don't have enough space, put your less-used items high on a closet shelf or in a storage box under the bed.

Now take another look at your closet. Do you need more clothes for casual days at work, a good raincoat with a removable lining for business travel, a basic suit that will serve you whether you're going to work or out to the theater? Draw up a shopping list. Be sure that you purchase easy-to-care-for clothing. If your toddler tends to wipe his jelly-smeared hands on your pants, then white is definitely not your color. Hate ironing? Skip cotton and go straight for the polyester blends.

To save the time you spend coordinating ensembles, buy complete outfits rather than separates and hang them together in your closet. When you can predict the weather as well as your schedule for the upcoming week, you might want to take time on Sunday to choose five outfits.

Hang them in order for Monday through Friday—that way it will take just a minute each morning to get dressed.

Streamline your grooming routine as well. A carefree hairstyle and simple makeup speed things up. If there's a line for the bathroom in the morning, consider showering the night before—the next day, all you have to do is brush your teeth, fix your hair, and shave or apply makeup.

If you have young children who need help dressing, avoid struggles by letting them choose their outfits, regardless of how badly their shirts and pants might clash. But be aware that too many choices can overwhelm some toddlers. Limit their options to two or three outfits, then let them choose the one they want.

A GOOD BREAKFAST

Do you go rushing out of the house each morning with nothing to eat—then succumb to the doughnuts a colleague has brought in? When you don't eat well, you shortchange yourself. You'll crash and burn by midmorning and fill yourself with sugar- and fat-laden junk food.

The first step in solving the problem is to plan breakfasts that are quick to prepare and healthful to eat. (No, these categories are not mutually exclusive!) Start by making a list of the nutritious foods that you and your family enjoy eating. Better yet, involve your kids and spouse in the process by having them make their own lists. Add the results to a standing master checklist that you can photocopy, add to, and take along to the store whenever you do your grocery shopping.

Use timesaving techniques: If your family loves waffles, make a batch on the weekend to freeze or buy the frozen kind and let your kids heat them in the toaster. Cook oatmeal in individual bowls in the microwave or add boiling water to the instant variety. Nonsugary cold cereals are just as nutritious as those you cook, and children can help themselves. When you truly don't have the time—or the stomach—to eat breakfast before you leave for the office, try bringing breakfast with you. Warm up a low-fat muffin in the microwave at work; pack yogurt, fruit, and a plain bagel; or keep cereal at your desk and milk and orange juice in the office fridge.

GETTING OUT THE DOOR

To cut down further on morning hassles, get organized the night before. Set up the coffeemaker so it's ready to turn on the minute you get up. Better yet, put it on a timer or buy a pot with a timer built in.

Plan tomorrow's routine before you go to bed: Have the children set out the clothes they'll wear the next day, including shoes and socks. Make sure all lunches are made and packed (if your kids are old enough,

> **Make a batch of waffles on the weekend to freeze or buy the frozen ones and let your kids heat them in the toaster.**

give this job to them). Decide on breakfast and set out whatever is not perishable. If you're someone who functions better in the morning, that's fine. Just be sure that you get up early enough so there is no need to rush—keeping in mind that your kids may not be morning people.

Dressing time *can be a chance for you and your kids to spend extra minutes together before going your separate ways.*

Speed through your daily departure by becoming an efficient time manager.

Gather your belongings—put any work you brought home into your bag or briefcase—and place your briefcase, umbrella, or anything else you need by the door. Remember to put your keys, wallet, and appointment book in your bag. Make sure your children do the same—homework, books, and permission slips go into the

backpacks. Consider building cubbyholes by the outside door. That way, everyone can place to-go items where they're easy to grab on their way out the door.

To motivate your kids and give them a clearer sense of what you expect of them, make and post a list of all they need to do in their daily routine—brush their teeth, make their beds, and other chores.

Use the Commute

If you travel by train or bus, carry the newspaper in your briefcase and read it on your way to work. This will keep you up-to-date and defuse frustration with traffic delays. On the way home, carry a folder of important reports, documents, and news articles to read. This will reduce your reading pile. Or just relax and make a list of things to do the following day.

GETTING TO WORK

Multiply the number of hours you spend traveling to work each week by the number of weeks in a year, and you'll realize how much valuable time you spend on this relatively unproductive activity.

If you take public transportation, use the opportunity to catch up on your professional reading, relax with a murder mystery, or even eat breakfast. If the ride is a half hour or more, you can get some work done and cut down on the time you spend in the office. Make sure you get a seat—if the bus or train is crowded and you have a choice of stops, try the earlier stop. You may be able to sit if you board there. A well-designed briefcase is invaluable if you plan on working en route: Make sure that it has room for your files and that you can open it easily while sitting in a bus or train seat.

If you drive, you can listen to books on tape or learn a foreign language, or dictate letters into a voice-activated tape recorder. You can use a cell phone to talk with customers or colleagues, but make sure that the conversation doesn't distract you from driving. Walk or bike to work as often as you can—it will take care of exercising and commuting at the same time.

If getting children to school is part of the routine, involve them in simplifying the process. Have them write their schedules on a large calendar to keep track of who needs a ride when and where.

Find out if there are alternatives to driving them. The school district may offer busing, or you might be able to set up a carpool with neighbors whose kids go to the same school. If your children are old enough, outfitting them with cell phones or pagers can be worth the cost— a change of plans won't leave you frantic.

When you have a choice of day care or schools, consider enrolling your children somewhere close to home or work. Eliminating an out-of-the-way trip can save time and irritation, especially in rush-hour traffic. Sharing the job with your spouse—particularly if you have staggered schedules—lightens the load. One of you can drop the kids off while the other picks them up. That way, you both can get in a full day's work without interruption.

A GOOD BAG OR BRIEFCASE WILL MAKE IT EASIER TO HAUL YOUR LOAD, WHETHER IT'S GYM CLOTHES, A LAPTOP, OR LUNCH.

◈

Sectioned tote
Are there many parts to your day? Here's a case that has it all: a compartment for your laptop, space for files and workout clothes, and a pocket for train tickets or a wallet.

Backpack
If your commute involves a long walk, a small backpack will ease the load without straining your shoulder. Be sure to get one that's lightweight and rainproof and has padded straps.

Laptop case
If you have a long commute, you can shave an hour off your day by working during the ride. With this case, you've got a portable office: Your computer and any important files are right at your fingertips.

DURING THE DAY

─────── ✴ ───────

TRY AS WE MIGHT, WE CAN'T ENTIRELY SEPARATE OUR WORK LIVES AND
OUR PERSONAL LIVES. WE MUST ATTEND TO ERRANDS DURING BREAKS,
MAKE PERSONAL PHONE CALLS, AND MEET WITH APPLIANCE REPAIR PEOPLE.

Although businesses are providing more services during after-work hours, you will still have some personal needs to handle between 9 A.M. and 5 P.M.

For some bosses, the only concern is that the work gets done. They don't feel the need to know your every coming and going. Others like to keep a tighter rein. Whatever the atmosphere at your workplace, it's best to be open with your supervisor so that he or she realizes you're not abusing company time. Almost all bosses will understand if you need to call a roofer after a storm blows your shingles off.

An occasional quick lunch *will let you touch base with coworkers and still have the rest of the midday hour to exercise or run errands.*

When you have to wait at home for the plumber to show up "sometime Tuesday morning," see if you can take some work with you the night before. If not, perhaps a neighbor or family member with a more flexible schedule can let the plumber in so you don't have to miss work. You can then return the favor by picking something up at the store for him or her.

One major boon to time-strapped employees is the advent of flextime—the option to adjust your work hours so that they fit better into your personal schedule. Whether your time crunch has to do with traffic, carpool needs, or school and day-care schedules, it might ease the pressure if you could work from 8 A.M. to 4 P.M. or 10 A.M. to 6 P.M. Even a company that

doesn't currently offer flextime might be willing to provide the option if asked—so give it a try. When you make your request, emphasize the ways you'll be more productive with the altered schedule.

If you don't have the luxury of a flexible schedule, you may need to be creative in your approach to running errands. Look for nearby businesses you can visit on your lunch hour or swing by on the way home (drive-throughs are speedy). Before leaving for an appointment, think about any errands that you may be able to complete on the same trip.

Sometimes it's more productive for you to take a personal day or sick day for an appointment. For instance, if the dog

Even a company that doesn't offer flextime might provide it if asked. Emphasize the ways you'll be more productive.

needs to go to the vet at lunchtime, do you really want to rush home to pick up Spot, race to the vet, head home to drop off the dog, and rush back to work? Instead, take the day off and try to attend to several other chores that are pending.

Personal phone calls can really eat into your work time. Maybe your mother always calls at 2 P.M., when her favorite soap finishes. Or a close friend who likes to chat about her problems phones you at the office every day because she knows you're a captive audience. Taking calls like this is a bad idea. Not only are you sabotaging any hope of getting all your work

Drive-Through Errands

If you drive to work, keep a basket in your car for videos and library books to return, film to develop, even discount coupons for take-out food you can pick up on the way home. Placing items in the basket is an easy way to remind yourself to drop off the tapes, books, or film, or to pick up dinner.

done during the day, but your boss and coworkers probably aren't too keen on seeing you gab away the afternoon.

Although it's hard to do, gather your courage and explain to those friends and family members that you can't chat during business hours. Promise to call them back after work or during a break.

QUICK, HEALTHY LUNCH

The leisurely, hour-long lunch break is fast becoming a thing of the past. Recent surveys have revealed that many of today's middle managers take less than a half hour to grab and eat their midday meal. Why? With so much to do in a day, many consider it a shame to waste a whole hour when they could be using the time productively—and taking that much less work home. Others—regardless of their place on the corporate ladder—feel the need to eat quickly so they have time to shop, exercise, or run errands.

Cooking Ahead

When preparing a favorite meal on a weekend, cook more than you need and freeze the leftovers in individual portions for the upcoming week's lunches. Meals that freeze well include lasagna, meat loaf, and stews. Avoid fresh fruit and vegetables as well as sandwiches with lettuce and tomato—they'll turn to mush in the freezer.

Recognizing this trend, restaurants, delis, and grocery stores have begun to add a variety of healthful to-go choices to their menus. Some also deliver or will let you call or fax ahead so that your lunch will be ready when you get there. Many lunch spots have salad bars priced by the pound. When you stop at the salad bar, you can fix two salads at a time and put one in the office refrigerator for tomorrow—just keep the dressing on the side. Or get an extra salad to take home for dinner.

If you bring your lunch from home, you don't have to spend an hour creating a gourmet delight. There are simple ways to eat healthfully and cheaply. Bring leftovers from last night's dinner. Shop for crackers and low-fat cheese in bulk, then add fresh fruit. If you don't mind always eating the same thing for lunch, you might take a loaf of bread to the office on Monday, along with some lunch meats, cheese, and condiments. You'll have the fixings for a fresh sandwich every day.

Whatever your tastes, try to limit yourself to a light lunch and a midafternoon snack. A big, heavy meal slows you down until your food is digested.

If you must eat at your desk, make it a meal you'll enjoy.

HOME, SWEET HOME

---✳---

AFTER WORKING ALL DAY, YOU'RE PROBABLY READY TO SIT BACK AND DO NOTHING WHEN YOU GET HOME. UNFORTUNATELY, HOUSEHOLD CHORES AWAIT YOU—COOKING, CLEANING, PAYING BILLS, AND SUPERVISING HOMEWORK.

Instead of feeling put-upon, get others to share the load. Solicit your family's ideas about ways to have everyone participate. If you have children, send them off to bed early enough so you have time to relax with your spouse. You've earned a rest!

KITCHEN TIME SAVERS

Feeding a family requires an incredible amount of energy and creativity. Keep it simple: Pick a few recipes that can get you through the week and make a shopping list. Some people designate each night of the week for a different food: fish night, pasta night, chicken night, and so on.

Shopping at the same store as much as possible will save time and frustration because you'll know just where to find everything. If you shop frequently, stick with a store that's conveniently located. If you prefer to do one major shopping trip a month, it may be worth driving a few miles to help out the budget. You'll still need a convenient place to pick up milk and other perishables more often. Some supermarkets have shopping and delivery services—some of them online—that may be worth their additional expense.

Other time savers in the kitchen:

Create a master grocery list. This is a great activity to do with elementary-school children. List all the items you normally keep on hand. Then make photocopies of the list to keep in the kitchen and check off things as you need them.

Give tasks to whoever gets home first. Post a list of jobs that need to be done before mealtime. There's no reason a spouse or older child can't cut vegetables, wash lettuce, shred cheese, or set the dinner table before the chief cook gets home.

Consider a monthly cooking marathon. Fix a big batch of spaghetti, a pot of soup, or a large casserole. Divide it into freezable portions you can microwave as needed. Always date any food container you put in the freezer so you'll use the oldest first.

Easy Does It

Collect recipes you can prepare with staple ingredients that are usually on hand—such as cheddar cheese, canned tomatoes, or frozen peas. Pick simple recipes with five or fewer ingredients that even children can manage. Make the weekday meals simple; leave the more challenging recipes for the weekends, when you're feeling adventurous.

SAVE TIME BY ROASTING A CHICKEN SUN-
DAY NIGHT AND USING THE LEFTOVERS
THROUGHOUT THE WEEK. SOME IDEAS:

Chicken pesto pasta

Start the linguine or spaghetti cooking, then
heat up a jar of premade pesto sauce. Toss
the pasta with the pesto and pieces of leftover chicken, and then add grated Parmesan
cheese. This dish goes well with a simple
salad of sliced fresh tomatoes, olive oil, and
freshly ground pepper.

Chicken curry salad

Combine curry powder with mayonnaise—
or yogurt for a low-fat meal—and mix in
small cubes of leftover chicken. Add apple
chunks, raisins, chopped celery, and nuts.
Line a salad bowl with lettuce and arrange
the salad on top. Serve with crackers.

Chicken tacos

Fill preformed taco shells with diced chicken,
avocado, lettuce, and pinto beans. Offer
bowls of salsa, sour cream, and shredded
cheese so that family members can prepare
the tacos to their own taste.

Keep your favorite take-out menus handy.
Stash them in a drawer or basket near the
phone, along with the restaurant's number.

Make snacks accessible but healthful.
If you've got young children who are constantly clamoring for snacks, designate a
low shelf in your refrigerator and pantry
as a place for nutritious snacks your kids
can grab when they're hungry: fruit, celery sticks, carrots. Also, keep easy-to-pour
containers of juice and water within reach,
along with some nonbreakable cups.

Let older children prepare some meals.
There's no rule that you and your spouse
need to do all the cooking. Assign the kids
to handle the cooking chores one night
a week. It will give you a break from the
daily routine, and it will help your children develop culinary skills.

COPING WITH PAPER

Do you get home from work so tired that
you can barely sort through all your junk
mail, let alone concentrate on paying the
bills? You can make the job easier by des-
ignating a place in the house that's con-
ducive to doing paperwork.

If you want to be able to watch the
children while you're working, a desk in
the kitchen or the family room may be
just the thing. On the other hand, if you
know that the only time you'll ever tackle
those bills is when no one's around, choose
a more private place. It doesn't have to be
a big space—just a comfortable one.

If you're the one who's responsible for
paying the bills, decide whether the best
method for you is to pay them as they
come in (not recommended by financial

Manage your after-work routine well and you'll have more time to play.

planners, but certainly better than no system at all) or at a regular interval such as weekly or monthly. If you're comfortable with computers, consider online banking options. Make sure to keep track of all the information you need for your tax returns.

In addition to paying bills, managing household papers—medical records, insurance documents, education records, and so forth—can also be a challenge. Nothing will create a household crisis more quickly than not being able to find a birth certificate for your 15-year-old who wants to sign up for a driver's education class at 8 A.M. tomorrow. It's essential—and it may even be lifesaving—to design a filing system so that other family members can find the information when they need it (see pages 76–79 for ideas on organizing files).

If you have children, you know that kids and paper go together. Help each child set up a system for managing schoolwork and artwork. Identify a specific place

to put important items that Mom or Dad needs to sign—a magnetic pocket on the refrigerator is a useful solution.

GETTING CHORES DONE

For evenings to run smoothly in a household of busy, working people, everyone—including the kids—needs to pitch in. If you haven't already done so, reach an agreement with your spouse about how you'll share the load. If the concept of taking turns with chores doesn't register with your spouse, try agreeing that each of you is responsible for certain tasks. You may discover that your spouse will be happy to cook if you'll do the shopping. But if one of you still ends up carrying most of the load and this is an ongoing cause of strife, consider whether that load even needs to be carried. Faced with an alternative of constant bickering, you may decide that it's fine that the floor doesn't get swept or the wastebaskets aren't emptied each night.

GETTING IT TOGETHER

---✳---

KEEPING YOUR FAMILY ON TRACK during the workweek can take some doing. These tools, which you can purchase at any hardware or housewares store, will save time and money, and they may even encourage everyone to take part in the organizing.

▲ **Make selecting chores** *more fun for young kids by writing them on strips of paper and hiding them in plastic eggs.*

▲ **Fill storage** *containers with casseroles, soups, and stews and freeze them for a quick lunch or dinner during the week.*

▶ **Purchase baskets** *for each family member and place them by the door. The night before, fill them with umbrellas, eyeglasses, mittens— everything that each member of the family needs for the upcoming day.*

◀ **Mount a large** *notepad on your refrigerator or a wall to post weekly chore assignments for the family or keep a running shopping list. Also useful is a whiteboard where the family can leave messages for each other. Or use magnets or pushpins to attach notes to a metal board or cork strip.*

Children need to do their homework and complete assigned chores without constant reminders. Set aside a time for homework and don't tolerate dawdling. If you're consistent and firm, your kids will not try to get out of their responsibilities.

To divvy up the chores, make a list of everything that needs doing; then solicit preferences. One kid might prefer to dust, another to sweep. Each child should have some daily chores—such as making the bed—but other chores can rotate.

Make it easy for others to help by relaxing your standards. Point out how much a young child is helping (even if he or she is scooping up cereal and half is still on the floor). Simplify household tasks as much as possible, particularly those that you delegate to the children. Compromise, not criticism, is the order of the day.

Sometimes it helps to provide an organizing tool. For example, if lost keys are a perennial problem in your household, a key holder with a spot for each person's keys may solve the problem.

Remember that streamlining your day is not a one-time event. No system can last forever, particularly when there are children involved—their abilities change. But once you've got the tools and the systems in place, maintaining the home routine will be much easier—and the satisfaction you get will carry over into your workday.

REJUVENATION

What a week! You've knocked them dead with your proposal, juggled more than a dozen important assignments, and kept your cool. Now it's time to reward yourself.

Reduce Your Paper Weight

Stay on top of the mail at home the same way you manage the flood of paper at work: Handle each item as few times as possible. Keep a basket nearby so you can recycle junk mail at once. Store your bills in one place and file away important papers the day they arrive.

Instead of feeling overwhelmed by the errands you've saved for the weekend, look for ways to restructure these days with the aim of maximizing rest and rejuvenation. Go over your to-do list to see what you can eliminate—perhaps instead of baking that cake for tomorrow's potluck, you can pick one up on the way home from the movie. Divide and conquer errands by delegating or trading tasks ("I'll go to the ATM if you can run by the dry cleaner"). Perhaps the Saturday outing could include a couple of errands before or after the main event.

Think about what you enjoy most and arrange to do it. If you love to read the paper or sleep late on Sunday mornings, ask the kids to play quietly so you can have some time for yourself.

Enjoy life's little pleasures. Buy flowers. Read an inspirational passage to nourish yourself. Take a bubble bath or have a long chat with an old friend. Sing a song. Enjoy your family and restore your soul.

BEING PART
of a **Team**

1 Be aware of how you present yourself to others. Your speech

and **body language** convey messages that you might not realize

you're sending. **2** Recognize that people of different genders and

nationalities have different **communication** styles. **3** Hone

your ability to **listen:** It's the most powerful communication tool you

have. **4** Try not to take **criticism** personally. Listen to it, learn,

and move forward. **5** Prepare before every meeting and **plan**

how to communicate your points most effectively. **6** Streamline

projects by defining **clear goals** and establishing a completion time

for each step. **7** Include different **personality types** on your

team in order to make it more effective. **8** Expect the best of

your employees. Most people will rise to your **expectations.**

9 Maintain **team morale** when conflict arises by dealing with

problems quickly, fairly—and on neutral ground. **10** Develop

effective team leadership skills through the best possible technique:

practice, practice, and more **practice.** ●

WORKING
WITH OTHERS

THE SIMPLE ART OF TEAMWORK

——————*

Whether you supervise others or you're on the team, clear communication is critical. If your nonverbal signals contradict your words, you may spend valuable time mending fences instead of getting things done. Clear, positive communication can streamline your work by reducing stress and building teamwork—a must for success.

Teamwork takes effort, but it's an effort well spent. If you can establish common goals, foster cooperation, and motivate other team members, your projects will move more quickly. Working with different types of people—sometimes people you find difficult—requires creativity and sensitivity, as well as effective negotiation and decision-making skills.

There are bound to be conflicts within any work group. Some will be easy to resolve, while others will demand more finesse. Finding a quick solution to a problem will help keep work on track and team members' morale high.

SAYING IT SUCCESSFULLY

---　✳　---

PROMOTING CONFIDENCE IN YOURSELF AND YOUR IDEAS IS ESSENTIAL TO ENSURING YOUR SUCCESS ON THE JOB, BUT EVEN THE BEST SUGGESTIONS MAY FALL ON DEAF EARS IF THEY'RE PRESENTED POORLY.

Just as advertisers sell a product by creating an enticing image, you can sell your ideas by delivering them articulately, professionally, and convincingly.

Body language unquestionably affects the way your message is perceived. Studies suggest that body language—not spoken words—conveys more than 60 percent of all information, so be aware of the signals you may be sending unconsciously. For example, crossing your arms can indicate an unreceptiveness to new information. Tapping your fingers or rattling the change in your pocket may convey boredom. Standing too close can be offensive, while standing too far away suggests aloofness.

Given today's global marketplace, more companies than ever before are dealing with multicultural staffs and international clients—which is why you need to be aware that body language differs from culture to culture. In Western society, for example, direct eye contact establishes rapport and sends an implicit message of confidence, honesty, and interest. Westerners may suspect that someone who doesn't look them square in the eye is not being completely truthful or is not very interested. But in many Asian cultures, looking away is a mark of respect, and direct eye contact is considered brazen. While changing one's style to match that of another culture is

Make your points effectively by selling them with style.

SIMPLE SOLUTIONS

IMPROVING THE CONNECTION

I F YOU FEEL YOU'RE JUST NOT clicking with a coworker, or if someone always seems to take things the wrong way, you'll need to find a new approach. Try framing your comments differently and take time to make sure that the message is understood.

Simple Ask the coworker to coffee or lunch. Say that the two of you seem to have a communication breakdown and that you would like to fix it. This may break the ice and open the way to a better relationship.

Simpler Take enough time to make your point clearly and explicitly. It can be tempting to speak quickly—especially if you feel uncomfortable—but your coworker may misinterpret your verbal shortcuts.

Simplest Approach the coworker differently—with a memo instead of voice mail, for instance. Perhaps he or she responds better at different times of the day, or in a different location, such as his or her own office.

---

not necessarily advisable, it's important to understand different styles in communication so you don't misinterpret them.

Cultural norms vary not only among nationalities or ethnic groups, but by age, race, religion, sexual orientation, physical ability, and gender. Much has been written about the disparate conversational styles of men and women. It's generally held that women are more concerned with making connections and creating consensus while men are more concerned with status and hierarchy. Because men and women may proceed from different assumptions, they may interpret the same conversation very differently. Being aware of these differences can help you choose your words.

A MATTER OF VOICE

Your voice is also crucial in communicating with authority. Have you ever listened to your answering machine message with surprise and said, "That doesn't sound like me"? (Or maybe you realize it does sound like you, but you don't like it.) Speakers of either sex whose voices are high-pitched, nasal, or breathy—vocal styles that tend to sound less authoritative—have to fight to overcome a negative impression every time they open their mouths. And people with foreign or regional accents find that some people are biased against them because of their manner of speech.

The easiest (and quickest) way to improve your voice "image" is to hire a good vocal coach. Check with your human resources department or the local Yellow Pages. If such services are unavailable or too expensive, consider using a program on cassette tape or CD. These programs offer a variety of exercises to improve your voice quality and style of communicating. Such training will make it much easier to get your point across.

It's unfair, but people also judge you by the way you dress—especially if you're meeting them for the first time. They'll jump to instant conclusions about your income, education, and status—even your intelligence—from the style and quality of your clothes. Although you might scoff at such superficiality, a well-chosen wardrobe can save you effort by silently convincing others of your authority.

you're in. The suit and tie that spell power at a brokerage may send out the wrong message at an advertising agency.

PREPARING YOURSELF

Adequate preparation is one of the best ways to take the stress out of any interaction. Mentally gearing yourself up hones your thinking and creates momentum. Before you meet with anyone—whether

Trying to understand the situation from the listener's point of view helps you anticipate possible objections.

To polish your image, take cues from the wardrobes of successful people at your workplace—if you come to work dressed like the boss, he or she may unconsciously start treating you as a peer. If you don't have a knack for putting outfits together, consult with a colleague or friend at work, or contact a personal shopper at a department store; their services are often free with a clothes purchase. Be sure to explain what image you're after and what field

it's with one person or an entire group—first determine just what you're trying to achieve, then think about the most effective way to accomplish your goals.

Suppose you want a raise and you've been stewing about it for weeks. You work up your courage at last, burst into your

Before any meeting, *take time to consider the best possible way to deliver the points you want to communicate.*

boss's office, and declare, "I've been here six months and I think it's time I got a raise." Clearly, this is not a great approach.

Take time to think. Request a meeting at the boss's convenience so that you can make your case calmly. Prior to the meeting, prepare a list of reasons why you feel your request is valid—a seminar that you conducted had 25 percent higher attendance than anticipated, for example, or the associate who had planned to leave the company decided to stay as a result of your assigning her to a challenging new project.

Rehearsing your position in advance and trying to understand the situation from the listener's point of view helps you anticipate possible objections and prepare to counter them. For example, suppose your boss says the current department budget won't allow a raise, even though she thinks you merit it. Be ready to ask if there are alternative ways you could be compensated, such as receiving stock options, participating in profit sharing, or taking off compensatory time.

ACTIVE LISTENING

Improving your communication skills requires more than saying the right words at the right time. It requires effective listening: hearing what is really being said so you understand the other person's position. All of us want to be understood. Your ability to communicate with others will improve significantly when you use techniques to show them they're being heard.

Active listening is one basic method for maintaining rapport in a conversation. This technique means you're participating

Talk Less, Listen More

Try to spend two-thirds of your time listening and one-third talking. (There may be a reason why we have one mouth but two ears!) Not only will you understand the conversation more fully, you'll also endear yourself to the other person. After all, everyone loves to be listened to.

in what the other person is saying, instead of just waiting for a chance to jump in. The way you do that is to clarify what she has just said. Try saying something like, "Let me see if I understand." Then recap what you heard. If the speaker agrees with your summary, ask her to continue. But if she indicates that you're not understanding, ask her to repeat what she has said until she agrees that your interpretation accurately represents her point of view. It's important to refrain from stating your opinion until you are certain you understand the other person's position.

Like any skill, active listening takes practice to master, but the payoff you get in building office relationships can prove phenomenal. It won't always work, but it's worth a try. It's handy when you need to nail down particulars. For instance, "We're relocating 45 employees and no one will lose their job. Is that correct?" Or if you think a colleague is being judgmental, critical, or inappropriately angry, repeat what he or she said. For example, suppose your boss says, "You always mess up when you work on this." Try repeating the statement: "You think I always mess up when I work on this." By doing so, you'll help the speaker hear the unfairness of the remark.

Another way to enhance communication is to "mirror" the other person's behavior, using his or her speech patterns and body language. Mirroring usually happens spontaneously when people are really listening to each other. When one person leans in to make a point, the second person often leans in as well, as if to hear better.

Tune in to the body language of others so you can pick up on how they're feeling. Showing sensitivity toward a colleague can promote cooperation or defuse a stressful situation. A simple comment such as, "It looks like you've got a lot on your mind today. Would it be better to make an appointment for another day?" communicates your real concern for the listener. The person may start paying more attention in return, or may choose to make another appointment. Either response is a step toward getting what you want.

Tune in to the body language of others. Showing sensitivity can promote cooperation or defuse a stressful situation.

Of course, the more you listen to people, the greater the chance you'll hear something you don't want to hear! The key is to try not to take it personally. Someone may make a remark tactlessly without intending any offense. If you're not clear about what the other person means, don't be afraid to ask. If your boss responds angrily when you've asked for help, you might say, "You sound frustrated with my request for a meeting tomorrow. Does that present a problem for you?"

ACCEPTING CRITICISM

When someone offers criticism, our first impulse is often to defend ourselves, which is rarely productive. Even if you disagree, acknowledge the criticism and try to clarify the issue. If a colleague dismisses your idea about reorganizing computer files, ask him to be specific about what he doesn't like. This will help everyone to talk about issues rather than personalities. When coworkers realize that they can speak openly and be heard, communication in the workplace becomes much more straightforward.

The Right Message

You'll get quicker results if you communicate in the medium that your coworkers are most likely to respond to. For example, if you notice that Jane responds readily to e-mail, make a note to use e-mail with her. If Bob, on the other hand, likes to meet in person, you'll find that you'll get an answer most quickly when you drop by his office.

THE DREAM TEAM

---✳---

HAVE YOU EVER WORKED ON A TEAM WHERE THINGS WENT SMOOTHLY MORE OFTEN THAN NOT, MEMBERS THRIVED ON MAKING EACH OTHER LOOK GOOD, EVERYONE GOT ALONG, AND THE WORK GOT DONE ON TIME?

If you've been lucky enough to have had this experience at least once in your career, you know the joy of effective teamwork.

For any team to succeed, its members need a common goal. They must rely on each other to achieve that goal and share in responsibility and accountability. When such a group of people comes together— or, more likely, is brought together by the exercise of sharp management skills—it eases the work of everyone involved.

So what sort of people make good team players? They are hard workers who are committed, dependable, and involved; people with knowledge, skills, or abilities relevant to the team's goal; good listeners who are supportive and cooperative as well as vocal, open, and honest; and flexible problem solvers who can adapt quickly to changing circumstances on the job.

Your ability to work as part of a team, whether you serve as a leader or as a rank-and-file team member, is crucial to your success in the workplace.

One simple way to become a valued member of a team is to expand your skills. If the person who used to input computer data just left the company, maybe you can

Outstanding team players coordinate their moves
and adapt quickly when the game changes direction.

Impromptu chats *at the water cooler or a group lunch can cement the bonds that help team members work together effectively.*

learn how to do the job. Reading a book or taking a professional class may not only be advantageous to you now, it could also further your career opportunities later.

Actions Speak Louder

Be part of the solution, not part of the problem. If you hear your coworkers complaining about the boss or the customer, don't add to the gripe session. Instead, try to clarify the issue by asking questions. Then offer constructive suggestions. Your coworkers probably don't realize they can change the situation.

When you need help, ask for it. It seems like so simple a thing to do that it's often dismissed. No one likes to look bad, and people will go to great lengths to cover up a situation that isn't going well.

If you've agreed to research the availability of critical specifications but have completely misplaced all your notes on resource contacts, confess the problem to the team leader. It's much more efficient than scrambling to reconstruct the contact list yourself and setting back the entire team two weeks. The team leader should know that everyone makes mistakes and will appreciate your honesty.

While there's no need to be best friends with every member of your office team, it is necessary to work together to achieve your goals. The more skillful you are in this arena, the greater your value to the team and to those in charge. Some alliances spring up informally around the water cooler or in the lunchroom. But in other cases, you may need to give a little nudge by inviting a colleague to lunch.

It's important for you to nurture an extensive in-house network of people supportive of one another's interests and goals.

IT TAKES ALL KINDS

In spite of your best efforts, teamwork is not always easy. Teams are made up of individuals who may have very different styles of working and communicating—and when styles clash, people often label each other as difficult, pushy, or worse. We tend to be most comfortable with people like ourselves and a little uneasy with those who work and communicate differently. We sometimes forget, however, that diversity brings necessary elements to the team and is often vital to success.

The people you work with won't seem nearly as difficult if you become aware of their strengths and weaknesses. Studies show that people can generally be divided into three major types: humanist, analytical, and goal-oriented. Humanist types

Breaking Rules

All teams may violate their own ground rules at times. For example, suppose a member of the team makes public preliminary results before all the data are in. If it happens repeatedly, your team needs to decide whether it's a problem and take action if it is. If breaking a rule doesn't interfere with the work or group dynamics, change the rule.

history with different vendors. A humanist is good at building effective teams and ensuring that differing opinions get aired. When a project is bogged down, the goal-oriented person often moves it forward. Working with others effectively is easy if you're aware of these personality types. It

While there's no need to be best friends with every member of the team, it is necessary to work together to achieve your goals.

want everyone to feel good and to enjoy the experience. Analytical types want to make sure the team has all the necessary information and has considered all the possibilities. Goal-oriented types want to reach the goal at all costs.

Making sure that a team includes all types of people is just good management. And because it's likely that such a group will get better results, the work is simplified. For example, an analytical type is the perfect person to research the company's

also helps to know that people have different ways of talking or dealing with others. Study the communication style of someone you're having trouble with. Maybe Joe comes across as brusque, but it's really just his manner of speaking. Perhaps Chris is simply shy rather than arrogant.

Communicating with coworkers—whether they're above or below you in the hierarchy—takes practice, practice, practice. If you need help, look for a mentor who is willing to offer you the benefit of

If You Can't Say Anything Nice...

When you're having trouble with a coworker, it's unwise to vent your displeasure by complaining about that person behind his or her back. Nothing erodes workplace morale more rapidly than the feeling that team members are spreading negative opinions about one another.

his or her experience in managing people. But if conflict ever reaches the critical stage—two team members disagree over everything just for the sake of argument, for example—the team needs to resolve the issue so that work can progress.

TALKING IT OUT

If it's necessary to confront a team member about an issue, make every effort to do so outside meetings. Present your case as objectively as possible, sticking with the facts and avoiding accusations.

For example, you can ask, "What did you mean specifically when you said the accounting department wasn't providing the information you needed? Our department met with your director several times to determine your department needs, so your statement is confusing to me." Then, when your coworker answers, really slow down and listen. You can easily defuse misunderstandings when you leave blame at

the door. Keep the focus on the problem and on finding the solution—not on each other or your individual styles.

Sometimes the simplest way to resolve a conflict is to get help from an outsider. A neutral third party, called a facilitator, sets the basic ground rules, such as no interruptions and taking turns to speak. He or she employs active listening, summarizing the position of each speaker in turn to be certain that positions and arguments are extremely clear. The facilitator attempts to bring into the open any hidden agendas that may be affecting the communication process. Since most conflicts result from a lack of understanding, hearing out the concerns of the opposition usually results in a more tolerant perspective and a greater likelihood of mutual agreement.

There are times, though, when people are just plain difficult. You've mustered all your tact and communication skills, and a colleague is still threatening the success of the project. Worse, he or she may be jeopardizing your career. Be careful about

You can easily defuse misunderstandings when you leave blame at the door. Keep the focus on the problem and solution.

going to the boss: You don't want to come across as divisive. And a person's failures will often reveal themselves. For example, if Ann consistently fails to meet her deadlines, and you and others pitch in to finish her research, you're encouraging her to continue the behavior—so stop helping.

A team normally works best when team members give each other a hand—but in this case, you need to correct a consistent problem. Ann's manager may not have realized that Ann was holding everyone up. Once he notices, he can correct the problem. The problem stays between Ann and her supervisor, and you haven't damaged your relationship with either of them.

TELLING THE BOSS

You might have to talk with your supervisor if other tactics don't work or if you find, for example, that a coworker has misrepresented your work. If that's the case, speak as diplomatically as possible and try to keep blame at bay. Say something like, "It came to my attention that you were told I did not update the team regarding the Williams project. I wanted you to know that I have been giving regular updates since March." If you're matter-of-fact about it, then your supervisor is less likely to see you as having a grudge.

Remember that all relationships in the workplace involve conflict from time to time. Some of that conflict is good: It shows that team members are testing new ideas and coming up with the best solutions to problems. If you've developed your sensitivity to group dynamics, you'll be able to ignore much of the conflict, and that in itself is a stress reducer.

If, however, you find yourself brooding over the unfairness, the stupidity, or the impossibility of a situation, you need to vent your frustrations in a positive way. You might talk about it with your spouse just to get it all out. Or draft a letter to your boss detailing your complaints, but don't mail it. Or take up yoga to relax.

If the situation doesn't improve, you'll need to address the problem directly. Talk

When you're *resolving differences with colleagues, try not to point fingers. Stay focused on the issues and listen carefully to the response. It's often just a misunderstanding.*

to your coworker about potential solutions. If things seem hopeless, one of you might ask to transfer to another team.

TAKING ON THE BOSS

Few of us are fortunate enough to have no one to report to, and maintaining a cordial relationship with your boss has a major impact on how easy it is to do your job.

Common courtesy goes a long way in smoothing relations with any supervisor: Being on time and flexible, having a good attitude toward customers and coworkers, demonstrating integrity, and being loyal to the boss and the company are essential to a healthy working relationship.

The fact is, most bosses want to keep and promote their staff because it means they'll get better results. When a boss loses a team member, the expense is staggering. It may cost a company hundreds or even thousands of dollars to refill a position.

If you're having trouble with your supervisor, approach him or her to discuss the problem. It may just be a misunderstanding or lack of information. Although it's scary to bring up uncomfortable subjects, it's almost always better to get them out in the open. Request a meeting and state your concerns. Most likely he or she will allay your fears and perhaps apologize for not communicating more effectively.

SERIOUS SITUATIONS

Sometimes, though, you'll run into a boss whose management techniques continually affect your job satisfaction despite your efforts to voice your concerns. Try talking with your company's human resources staff. They may have experience with this particular supervisor or some ideas on how to manage a difficult manager. If everyone on the staff is unhappy with the supervisor, you may want to risk gathering the team and asking the boss for a meeting. The boss is more likely to listen when everyone expresses the same concerns.

You'll want to go over your supervisor's head—as a group or individually—only in very serious cases such as discrimination,

Although it's scary to bring up uncomfortable subjects, it's better to get them out in the open. Ask to meet and air your concerns.

sexual harassment, or behavior that's abusive or demeaning. Document incidents so you'll have concrete examples to offer.

When you've done all you can to resolve a problem with your boss, you may have to find a new position. Unfair as it may seem, chances are the company values your boss more than it values you: A higher-level employee has more experience and is far more difficult and expensive to replace. If you like the company, you may be able to find another position internally.

If you decide to leave before finding another job, you may be able to negotiate a severance package. Companies want employees to depart on good terms and may pay a few months' salary.

Whatever you decide, there's no sense in staying if you're unhappy. You'll lose confidence in yourself and your abilities, and that will hinder you in the long run.

EFFECTIVE MANAGEMENT

---- ✳ ----

WHEN YOU'RE THE ONE IN CHARGE, WHETHER OF A PROJECT, A TEAM, OR A WHOLE DEPARTMENT, YOUR ABILITY TO LEAD OTHERS, DELEGATE TASKS, PLAN PROJECTS, AND TRACK THEIR PROGRESS IS CRITICAL TO YOUR SUCCESS.

As team leader, you're responsible for supplying the glue that binds the group and the focus that keeps it on track. Hone your management skills well and you'll streamline everyone's job—including your own.

Effective team leaders provide strong guidance and direction while the team is developing its identity and ways of working together; then they gradually delegate responsibilities once the project has gotten off the ground. A team that performs at a high level can rotate leadership for specific projects among various members of the team.

Your challenge is to coach the team and bring out the best in each member. Strive for the following objectives:

Develop a positive vision. Consider the example of the circus tightrope walker: He or she learns to focus on reaching the other side, not on avoiding a fall.

Expect the best of others. If you provide clearly defined expectations for the group, most people will rise to meet them.

Look at long-term results. People find it easier to overcome short-term roadblocks when they are able to see the big picture.

Motivate your team to reach the objective by setting interim goals.

Always use your best manners. When you're the head of the team, you can never say please and thank you too often!

A GOOD LEADER

Excellent leaders are visionaries who have superior people skills; they are adept at communicating the big picture and motivating their teams. Although some individuals undoubtedly are born leaders, the rest of us have to develop the necessary

To build a team that does the best possible job—while remaining loyal to you and the group—follow these watchwords:

Be honest. Tell the truth at all times—diplomatically and discreetly, of course. Instead of saying, "I know nothing about the upcoming merger," say, "I can't discuss it until the president gives me permission."

Be loyal to your staff. If your boss complains about mistakes in a report from your office, don't blame your secretary.

Research shows that by admitting errors, you often build greater trust because you're seen as a collaborator, not a competitor.

skills through training and experience. Most people don't wake up one day knowing how to conduct an effective meeting, for instance. Instead, we observe others who do it successfully, think about what works and what doesn't, and study tools and techniques to improve our skills.

Bad News Is Good to Know

Consider making it a team goal to avoid unpleasant surprises through open communication. Let team members know that the bearer of bad news won't be punished. The sooner everyone knows of a bad situation, the more likely the team can find a solution before it's too late.

Be fair. It establishes your credibility and helps people to accept unpopular decisions. Don't allow one person comp time and deny another the same opportunity.

Practice what you preach. If you expect others to take risks, be willing to take a risk yourself. If you want your staff to admit mistakes, admit your own. Research shows that by admitting errors, you often build greater trust because it helps others see you as a collaborator, not a competitor.

Pitch in when necessary. The members of your team will respect you if you help occasionally with the small stuff.

Remember to laugh. Nothing gets you through a crisis like a sense of humor.

Involve your staff in decisions. Involving people in choices whenever possible increases their sense of accountability and their incentive to get the job completed. For example, ask a subordinate when she anticipates the survey will go out. If you see a problem with the date she suggests, work out a compromise. Ask: "Will that give you time to collate the information?" Help her arrive at a date she's comfortable with rather than assigning her a date.

ASSIGNING TASKS

A skilled team leader knows how to delegate. Effective delegation creates a strong team spirit and allows you to accomplish more with less effort in less time.

Often, the person to whom you have assigned the task may not perform it as well or as quickly as you could, but don't fall into the trap of doing it yourself. Suppose you need to write a letter. If you ask an assistant to write it and you have to revise 80 percent of it, you may initially lose time, but you'll have given someone a chance to improve his or her skills. Each time that person writes a letter, he or she will get better at it, and eventually you'll make minimal changes or none at all.

Let your staff put their own spin on an assignment and allow them to learn from their mistakes. From this they'll gain a deeper understanding of the assignment. Once you've delegated tasks, be sure to give the team the tools it needs to do the job. Allocate the necessary time and resources to employees, train team members adequately, and be sure to provide regular feedback, praise, and recognition. In time you'll learn to master the art of monitoring your employees' progress while giving them the room they need to grow.

PROJECT MANAGEMENT

A project manager is often a team member who has been assigned to lead a particular project. If this is your situation,

Delegating Decisions

In some cases a team leader may ask another member to make a decision. This works well when the decision requires particular expertise or when time is short. For example, you might tell the group, "Ruth and Frank will be responsible for getting input from everyone on the team, but they will make the final call on which supplier to use."

you'll find that being in the lead is a bit tricky: You'll have to use persuasion rather than coercion to reach your goals.

At the same time, you need to make quick decisions. Most important, you need to give your team a specific objective. Until you define objectives, determine goals, and set time frames, it's impossible to monitor a project's progress. If your team members don't know where they're going and when you expect them to get there, they can't know if they're on track. Your team's objectives should meet the following criteria:

The goal must be clear. The team has to know exactly what must be achieved.

The goal must be measurable. The team should be able to define this achievement with objective criteria such as dollars saved or percentage of production increased.

The goal must be agreed upon. The team should determine the objective and be able to define the desired results before embarking on the project.

Simply Put...

Chart Talk

Gantt chart • Invented for the U.S. government by Henry Gantt during World War I, this tracking tool is a time line that shows starting and ending dates for tasks. It creates a visual display of simultaneous events.

PERT chart • A Project Evaluation and Review Techniques (PERT) chart looks like a collection of boxes connected by arrows. Each of the boxes represents a task; the arrows represent relationships between those tasks. A PERT chart can be linear, or it can branch out and return to a final point.

Include the members of your team in the decision making whenever possible. Ask them to let you know immediately if they anticipate any problems in meeting the project's deadlines.

As team leader, it's your job to keep the goal in the team's sight. Members of a team—and leaders—often become sidetracked by less important details. Remind those on your team of the goal by asking them frequently how their work is progressing. If they talk about a side issue, steer them toward the goal.

A firm deadline and interim checkpoints will help to keep everyone on track. Determine a realistic target date and work backward to identify goals along the way, such as writing the first draft of a report or creating a working prototype.

In addition to making sure the job gets done on time, you may be expected to document progress in regular reports to management. Meet periodically with individuals to whom you've delegated tasks, or hold group meetings to share information that will become the basis of your report.

A good tracking tool will help you keep everything on course. You can track less complicated assignments in your calendar or personal planner. But for a more complicated assignment, draw up a chart such as a Gantt or PERT chart. Specialized software that includes these charts can help you track and report the team's progress on complex projects. Also, note major deadlines in your calendar so you'll know to monitor the project's status.

Regardless of what tracking tool you use, don't wait until the deadline is upon you to uncover the snags and delays that can threaten your project's successful outcome. Helping team members stay on track is a major role of a good leader. Let them choose their own tracking system but have them update you frequently.

RESOLVING CONFLICT

If you establish goals clearly, delegate work fairly, and set a positive example, you'll inspire subordinates to perform at their best. But even the most seasoned bosses have to address problems with employees or conflicts between two subordinates.

No matter what the problem, it's important to address it before it escalates. If a team member consistently arrives late, for instance, speak to the person about it as soon as possible. If you don't, he or she may start arriving later and later, tardiness may hold up a project, and coworkers may grow frustrated that you haven't addressed the situation. Acting quickly ensures that the entire team stays productive.

Stay flexible in your approach to each situation. Don't assume that you always need to assert your authority or that you

If two or more employees are at loggerheads, meet to discuss the problem. Give everyone equal time to speak.

must keep everyone happy. Every situation calls for a different resolution. If an employee asks for time off just before a crucial deadline, for example, you might compromise and give her extra time after the deadline is met. On the other hand, if two team members haven't solved a disagreement about a presentation that's scheduled to begin in 30 minutes, you'll

have to make a quick call. In rare cases, it may make sense to ignore a problem. For example, if a normally reliable employee takes an unusually long lunch one day, it's probably best to forget it.

If two or more employees are at loggerheads and the tension is affecting productivity, you'll have to step in and resolve the fight. Set a time when all of you can meet and discuss the problem; make sure the meeting area is in a location that's informal and is neutral territory, such as an empty office or a conference room.

Ask questions, giving each party equal time to speak. Get all the details but keep the discussion under your control so it doesn't disintegrate into accusations. Once you understand the problem, ask everyone for help in finding a solution, then make certain that everyone agrees with it.

A team that works *out methods for resolving conflict will remain on good terms even after completing a highly stressful project.*

DON'T AGONIZE,
Organize

———✳———

1 Clear out the **clutter** from your work area to provide both physical and mental space. **2** Consider the **image** you want your office to reflect about you and your work. **3** Create a place that **energizes** and soothes you with a combination of functional and inspirational items. **4** Identify the specific **tools** you need to keep your work progressing smoothly—and keep them right at hand. **5** Manage the deluge of daily **mail** by deciding immediately whether you should file it, act on it, or toss it. **6** Create a highly functional **filing system** as a place to hold anything you or your colleagues might need in the future. **7** Transform scraps of paper into powerful **resources** with an effective card file. **8** Make use of action files to keep your projects **moving** steadily toward completion. **9** Set up a **file index** and keep it handy to help you and your coworkers find documents quickly. **10** Date all your files and then review them regularly—keep clutter down by **tossing** files that are outdated or no longer useful to you. ●

ORGANIZING
YOUR OFFICE

**EASY WAYS TO MAKE
YOUR WORK SPACE WORK**

＊———＊———＊

Your work space is your base of operations. If it's well designed, it will boost your productivity. But if your desk and furnishings are not pleasant and comfortable, if your desk is so cluttered that you can't find what you need, if papers enter your office and never seem to leave, you'll be neither happy nor productive on your job.

How do you find the time to get organized? When your work is piling up and the phone is ringing nonstop, it may seem crazy to steal time for such a seemingly unproductive task. But be aware that you'll end up spending much more time searching for lost memos and business cards if everything is stacked haphazardly on your desk and randomly stuffed into drawers. An hour spent organizing your work space today will save you many hours of frustration later and will make it much easier to keep clutter at bay.

HOME AWAY FROM HOME

———— ✳ ————

DURING A TYPICAL WORKWEEK, THERE'S A GOOD CHANCE YOU SPEND MORE WAKING HOURS IN YOUR OFFICE THAN AT HOME, SO WHY NOT MAKE IT A PLACE WHERE YOU CAN FUNCTION EFFECTIVELY AND FEEL COMFORTABLE?

Whether your work space is a posh corner office, a cramped cubicle, or a desktop out in the open, make it work for you rather than against you. The steps are straightforward: Eliminate everything that's extraneous, organize what remains, and then add a few well-chosen personal touches.

The most powerful action you can take to simplify your work space is to banish all the unnecessary clutter. If you inherited your office from someone else, you may feel guilty about getting rid of anything. But do you really need your predecessor's card file full of outdated contacts or a collection of novelty pens from

last year's trade show? Perhaps you've accumulated some "treasures" of your own, such as the outrageous plastic flower display you won at the office white elephant party. Just imagine how energized you'd feel, and how much easier it would be to focus and concentrate, if the entire unappealing mess were to suddenly disappear.

Even if you do manage to be efficient in a disorganized office, it requires much more effort on your part. And consider what your work space says about you to coworkers and customers. If your desk is so buried in paper that colleagues have to tape messages to your monitor to make

Give your office a personal touch and you'll feel happier spending time there.

sure that you'll see them, a visitor will not be inspired to trust you, no matter how abundant your talents may be.

CLEARING THE DECK

Ready for action? Take a deep breath and start paring down your work space to the essentials. Look hard at each object and ask yourself the following question: Is this a necessary tool *for the job I have now?* If the answer is no, then the object doesn't belong in your office. Take it home, give it away, or simply trash it.

To qualify as a keeper, an item must also be in good repair. The lamp that blinks on and off is not doing much for your concentration. Replace or repair it so you can get on with your work.

There's one important exception to this rule: Hold on to the things that motivate you, inspire you to excellence, and remind you of why you go to work—photographs of your children, the achievement award you received last year, or a brochure for the mountain getaway you're heading to for vacation.

MAKING YOUR MARK

After you've discarded the superfluous and nonfunctional, take a look at what's left. Some offices tend to have efficient but heartless cookie-cutter work spaces. Nonetheless, this space is yours. If your supervisor allows, create an ambience that is both stimulating and soothing.

Choose only a few simple things that make you feel good. They'll have an impact on your happiness—not to mention your productivity—at work. Vivid

Share the Wealth

If you have difficulty parting with something you no longer use or have too much of, find someone else who needs it more than you do. Designate a shelf in the supply closet for reusable items such as picture frames, vases, coffee mugs, plant holders, and so on. Knowing they'll find a new home will make it easier for you to let go of them.

colors and bold designs may suit you perfectly, while your neighbor across the hall may prefer pastels and muted lines. Maybe you'd like to post inspirational quotes about teamwork, courage, and success—or photo enlargements from your ski vacation. Whatever you choose, make sure it's consistent with the company image. And consider that each item of decoration—from the pictures on the wall to the paraphernalia on your desk—makes a statement about you. Be sure it's the message you want to convey.

When it comes to personal belongings, less is definitely more. Instead of a mishmash of family photographs, choose just one or two to display tastefully on a shelf. As your children get older, update your small display and retire the earlier versions. The goal isn't to produce a silver-frame-on-the-piano effect but to create an opportunity to connect with the people who matter the most in your life.

A SPACE OF YOUR OWN

✦

I T'S SURPRISING HOW LITTLE YOU NEED to turn a functional but drab work space into a user-friendly work environment. A few simple touches can make your office feel more like home—and organize your papers and equipment at the same time.

▲ **Bring containers from home** *to serve as creative alternatives to the standard-issue pencil cup.*

▲ **A potted plant** *can provide greenery and privacy in a crowded office. Consider the level of available light before choosing a plant.*

▲ **This wooden carryall** *gives your work space a hint of old-fashioned charm.*

▶ **Your in box** *and out box don't have to look like everyone else's. Try hanging a pair of baskets on the wall near your desk.*

Bringing nature into your indoor environment can give you a boost as well. Most people find the sound of running water soothing and energizing, so it's not surprising that one of the latest decorating rages is to use small, self-contained fountains or aquariums. A well-chosen plant can instantly transform your space, too, providing an atmosphere of welcome and warmth. Be certain to match the plant's light requirements with what's available, or it will soon be yellow, leggy, or dead.

Rather than surrounding yourself with a jumble of small plants, consider one well-placed larger specimen in a decorative container. If real plants aren't an option in your office, a travel bureau may be happy to provide you with beautiful posters of lush landscapes. Or create your own artwork by enlarging favorite photographs.

POWER PLACEMENT

For thousands of years the Chinese have applied the gentle influence of *feng shui* (pronounced "fung shway"), the ancient art of auspicious design. This age-old folk wisdom may well enhance your feeling of personal power in your work space.

Feng shui prescribes certain placements of furniture in a room. In particular, the relationship of your desk and chair to the door is important. The "position of power" is at a diagonal from the entrance, where you have full view of the doorway at all times. This vantage point allows you to monitor and control the entrance to your work space and to reduce the likelihood of being startled by visitors—a situation that is said to diminish your *chi* (cosmic

Greenery Aloft

Plants in your office help improve your mood—and your health, as they absorb carbon dioxide and indoor pollutants while releasing oxygen. Some offices lend themselves easily to the hanging of plants from sturdy pipes along the ceiling— an ideal way to add greenery without taking up space on desks or other surfaces.

energy). If positioning your furniture this way means you can no longer take advantage of a cherished window vista, consider using a mirror on the opposite wall to bring it back into view.

When there are two or more desks in a room, with the potential for ongoing distraction and annoyance, devotees of *feng shui*—as well as many office interior designers—recommend the judicious placement of dividing screens and large plants between desks. These physical barriers redirect what *feng shui* calls negative energy and encourage harmony and focus.

YOUR COMFORT ZONE

Whether or not you accept the principles of *feng shui,* some furniture arrangements are inherently more efficient than others. For example, a U-shaped arrangement of desk, side table, and files allows the most working surface. Another arrangement that provides substantial working surface

Watch Your Back

Adjust your chair properly (and change its position from time to time) to avoid aches and pains. Check out your local office-supply store for back support pillows that adjust to fit you personally. If possible, create an area in your office where you can work standing up from time to time; it will take a lot of stress off your back.

repetitive stress injuries. The monitor should be directly in front of your eyes so you don't have to strain your neck to view the screen. Your keyboard should be low enough so that when you type, your elbows are at right angles. If you still find typing uncomfortable, inquire whether your company will pay for an ergonomic keyboard. These keyboards are angled to fit your hands more naturally.

SAFE SEATING

A good chair can be a lifesaver. Your chair's seat, backrest, and armrests all should be adjustable to fit you comfortably. A chair that swivels left and right, rolls on casters, and tilts forward and backward will also move with you. This will prevent you from straining your back as you reach for files or pens or a dropped document.

is the L shape (traditional secretarial desk), a particularly good solution for a corner. Figuring out the most effective positioning of your office furniture will pay off in a more economical use of your energies.

You should also make sure your computer equipment is positioned correctly—otherwise, you could be hampered by

It's also important to make sure that your telephone and your most-used files and supplies are within easy reach. To determine whether your work space is as

A comfortable chair puts you in a good mood while
you're working. Make sure yours adapts to your needs.

convenient as it could be, sit in your chair and stretch out an arm, sweeping it across your desk. Everything you use the most frequently—phone, pens, pencils, writing pad—should lie within easy grasp of your right hand if you're right-handed or your left hand if that's your dominant hand.

ORDER! ORDER!

Even the best ergonomic chair and a well-positioned desk won't help you if your desktop is so littered with papers that you can never find what you need. If the clutter has gotten out of control, you may despair of knowing where to begin.

The first step in bringing order to the chaos is to designate one section of your desk as a sorting area and remove all the papers from that area. Use the cleared space to group like items in piles: articles and reports in one pile, correspondence in another pile, invoices in a third, and so

An ergonomic chair *will make your life easier—and protect your back. Choose one that swivels, rolls, and is fully adjustable.*

into your already-stuffed pen holder, computer documentation you borrowed from the office software library. Place these in a big cardboard box and return them to their respective storage areas.

Figuring out the most effective positioning of your office furniture will pay off in a more economical use of your energies.

forth. Also sort supplies: paper clips, unused file folders, sticky notes, computer disks. As you sort, weed out the items that you know you'll never need or that you can get elsewhere. Into this category fall price sheets from suppliers you don't deal with often and correspondence from casual business associates you know you'll never see again. Throw them away.

Now decide what doesn't belong on your desk or even in your office: loose-leaf notebooks you took from the supply room but never use, extra pens that won't fit

Finally, look through the sorted stacks that remain. Some papers, including articles you may want to read later, belong in established files; put them there now. Others may form new categories—they've accumulated on your desk because you didn't know where to file them in the first place. Make file folders for these documents (see page 76) and stow them away.

Virtually every work space will benefit from having an in box, an out box, and a to-file box. These "boxes" can be trays, baskets, wooden or wire containers, or any

Identifying a proper place for everything— *and devising a system to keep it there—can prevent desktop clutter from creeping back once you've organized your office.*

other type of sturdy receptacle—as long as they serve their purpose of keeping the paper flow under control.

Make the in box the place where co-workers can put your mail and new assignments. The out box is for items that have to go elsewhere—to coworkers' offices or into the mail. Locate the out box in a spot that's convenient for you and the person who picks up its contents for delivery. The to-file box holds items that are waiting for you to file them away. It's more efficient, generally, to file several papers at once than to file them one at a time.

Once you've conquered your desktop, use the same process to tame the chaos in your desk drawers: Empty them, then sort, discard, and put everything in its proper place. It may help to use drawer organizers to keep the pieces in order.

Now that your work space is clear of paper, it's time to set up a system that will keep it that way. Physics defines *entropy* as "the natural and irreversible tendency toward randomness and disorder in any system without an external source of energy." In the case of your desk, *you* are the external source of energy. No one else will put that stapler back in its place!

Follow these rules to decide where to stash the items that pile up on your desk:

♦ IF YOU USE IT DAILY, IT CAN LIVE ON TOP OF YOUR DESK.

♦ IF YOU USE IT WEEKLY, IT CAN LIVE INSIDE YOUR DESK.

♦ IF YOU USE IT MONTHLY, IT CAN LIVE IN YOUR OFFICE.

♦ IF YOU USE IT LESS THAN MONTHLY, IT CAN BE PUT IN OFF-SITE STORAGE.

Let's face it—some of us will never be neatniks. But that doesn't mean we need to let chaos take over. The key to staying organized is never to let the mess get out of hand. Start with a workable setup, and it will be easier to maintain.

THE DAILY NITTY-GRITTY

OK, YOU'VE FINE-TUNED YOUR WORK SPACE, FOUND A PLACE FOR THE ESSENTIALS, AND ELIMINATED ALL THE UNNECESSARY CLUTTER. ARE YOU STILL FEELING OVERWHELMED BY THE PAPER THAT PILES UP DAY AFTER DAY?

The next step is to set up simple systems that allow you to manage your desktop, keeping work flowing smoothly from your in box to your out box.

For most jobs, there is no right or wrong way to get the work done—what counts are the results. To streamline your methods, ask yourself whether a technique is effective and to your liking. If not, a change is clearly in order. For example, if you never miss appointments because you faithfully record them in your calendar but you frequently misplace phone numbers, the solution is to identify one place where you will consistently put the phone numbers, such as a rotary card file.

If what you do or don't do has an impact on other people, ask yourself whether your system works for others. You may take pride in being able to find everything in your office—in spite of how it looks. But what happens if you're home sick tomorrow? As an employee, you're responsible for organizing your work so someone else could take over if need be.

How many times have you walked into your office and cleared off your desk only to find yourself swimming in paper by day's end? Maybe you're taking the wrong approach: Rather than cleaning up periodically, develop a better system for keeping your work moving through your

hands. The best way to keep your desk clean is to prevent the papers from piling up in the first place. Let's take a look at how you can set up a system that will work for you and for your company.

PREVENTING CLUTTER

It's no secret that clutter results from postponed decisions. Decide what to do with each piece of paper as it arrives, and you'll keep clutter at bay. The good news here is that there are only three decisions you can make about any piece of information, whether it's electronic or paper: File it away

If you act on papers *as soon as they land in your in box, you'll keep your desk clean and move your projects forward. A desk free of paper lets you work and think clearly.*

All in One Place

Keep a notebook handy for jotting down all kinds of information you glean throughout the day: phone messages, notes from conversations, items that come up at meetings. This will keep your desk clear of numerous small scraps of paper. Mark the action items with a star, and then transfer them once a day to your to-do list or calendar.

With computers and copiers in almost every office, it's easy to give information to everyone. But just because you received a piece of paper doesn't mean you need to keep it. Ask yourself these questions: Does this paper require my action? Do I have a specific purpose for it? Would it be difficult to get again? Do any company guidelines require me to keep it?

If the answers are no, put it in the wastebasket or recycling bin immediately. You can eliminate reminders such as meeting notices by transferring the information to your calendar or to-do list.

TRIMMING THE TO-DOS

But what about all those papers you really do need to keep on hand? Although the adage "Handle a piece of paper only once" sounds great in theory, it's not practical unless you can complete everything that comes your way by the end of the day. You can at least resolve to move everything out of your in box after handling it once. To do that, you'll need to set up a sensible system so you can retrieve each item at precisely the time you need it.

Initially, you can divide the papers you need into two major categories: those that require action and those that need to be filed away for future reference. Every paper that requires activity on your part needs to go into an action file. Keep these files close at hand. Some will be for short-term actions, such as a trip or a report.

Other tasks are ongoing—you might need an action folder for "Data Entry," "Photocopying," "Discuss With…," or "Phone Calls to Make," for example. As

for future use, act on it, or toss it (preferably into the recycling bin). Keep these three options in mind with the acronym FAT: file, act, toss. (And always consider the last option first!)

If your mailbox lies down a hallway from your cubicle or office, screen your mail before taking it back to your work

Ask yourself: Does this paper require my action? Do I have a specific purpose for it? Would it be difficult to get again?

space. Typically you can discard almost half of your mail, so be ruthless. Reroute as much as possible on the spot, into the trash, the recycling, or a coworker's box if that's where it belongs. If space allows, position a large wastebasket and recycling bin close to the mailboxes to encourage everyone else in your office to use them.

UNCLUTTERING YOUR DESK

C ONQUERING DESKTOP CLUTTER is the key to creating an efficient work space—and to projecting an aura of calm control even when you feel panicked. Use accessories such as these to keep tools and papers out of your way, yet still at hand.

▲ **Keep paper under control** *by affixing important notes to a tackboard for easy reference. Stacking bins can hold papers you need to file or act on.*

▼ **Stay organized anywhere** *with a rolling file cabinet. Office supplies are handy but hidden in its segmented drawer insert; color-coded folders help you locate project files in a flash.*

▲ **Wall-mounted hot files** *will keep essential papers at your fingertips while freeing up precious space on your desk.*

▶ **Need a pencil right now?** *A revolving tray for pens, pencils, scissors, tacks, and clips keeps everything centrally located and easy to grab in a hurry.*

If you can't find a document in a matter of minutes, you need a new filing system.

you look at each piece of paper in your in box, transfer it directly into the appropriate file if it requires you to take action.

Creating a separate file for each type of task will allow you to handle similar activities all at once. For instance, if you're

When it comes to work spaces, there are two kinds of people: those who want everything visible and those who want everything put away.

making a phone call, you can probably make another one very quickly if all the papers you need are right there. Or you might want to delegate the week's photocopying to an assistant.

Every job has actions specific to that position. An insurance customer-service representative might have a file labeled "Waiting for Reply From Underwriting," while a sales representative would have one titled "Waiting for Check."

The beauty of this system is its simplicity. Often people procrastinate because a piece of paper reminds them of several actions they need to take, and they may feel overwhelmed. For example, a letter may require a response, but you must first make a phone call to verify some details, which then need to be discussed with another team member (who is out of town). Instead of throwing the paper back in a pile, ask yourself: What is the next action I need to take? In this case, you need to make the phone call, so file it in the folder labeled "Phone Calls to Make."

You may find it helpful to set aside a specific time each day to handle phone calls and other specific actions. When the hour arrives, just pull out the appropriate folder and get busy. If there's a call you need to make at a different time of day, put a note on your calendar or to-do list.

RIGHT VERSUS LEFT

When it comes to managing a work space, there are only two kinds of people—those who like to have everything out on their desktop at once, and those who want to have everything put away. Each method has advantages and drawbacks.

People who prefer everything out in the open tend to be visually oriented. Seeing the work in front of them reminds them of what they need to do. In fact, they may fear that if it's out of sight, it's out of mind. These types of people, often referred to as right-brained thinkers, tend to be intuitive and creative, skilled at handling several tasks at once. But they often let clutter build up to the point where it interferes with their work.

In contrast, individuals who are left-brained are likely to think in linear ways. The A-to-Z labels in traditional filing cabinets make perfect sense to them, but having too many unfinished projects pending at once leaves them frazzled.

How do you know which category you're in? People with left-brain dominance find it natural to put away papers they're not using and to toss out unneeded items as they go along. They also tend to make lists and put reminders in writing. They are more time-conscious, and they set goals and plan ahead carefully, preferring to do one thing at a time.

On the other hand, people with right-brain dominance prefer to stack important papers all around them as visual reminders; use baskets and bags instead of files; and maintain lots of resource materials, such as magazines and newspapers. They keep their to-do lists in their heads. They're also less time-oriented, acting spontaneously rather than sticking to a schedule, and feel comfortable juggling many balls at once.

If you're a right-brainer, you can benefit from using color-coded notebooks, file folders, sticky notes, and highlighters. You may also prefer open storage systems, such as bookshelves divided into sections. If you're left-brained, have plenty of folders, file drawers, drawer organizers, and labels so you can put everything away.

Regardless of which side of your brain predominates, a trip to an office-supply store can help. You'll find more solutions to organizing office clutter than you ever knew existed; one of these might be just what you were looking for.

Many Happy Returns

Create a "Calls Expected" file for information you'll need when someone returns your call. Then you can quickly grab the file as soon as the phone rings. If you need to get a return call from, say, John in time for a meeting or an appointment, mark your calendar on the day before with "John—CE" (call expected). This will remind you to follow up if John doesn't call.

FINDING IT FAST

---✳---

INFORMATION IS POWER—IF YOU CAN PUT YOUR HANDS ON IT WHEN YOU NEED IT. TURN YOUR STACKS OF PAPER INTO POWERFUL RESOURCES BY CREATING, IMPLEMENTING, AND MAINTAINING AN EFFECTIVE FILING SYSTEM.

If you think that filing is low priority, or that it has little to do with streamlining your work, think again. Research shows that the average worker spends 150 hours per year looking for misplaced information. A filing system that works efficiently can make you the office star.

Does your filing system swallow papers like a black hole? Are you still struggling with a system you inherited from someone else but have never cleaned out? If it's impossible to locate what you want easily in your filing system, don't waste your time trying to file any more papers. Your best bet is to start over.

Skip the Clip

Avoid using paper clips in files whenever possible. They take up twice the space that staples do, and they're notorious for catching on unrelated papers and slipping off, never to be seen again. Instead, remove the clips as you file away papers, using staples instead. Keep your stapler and a staple remover within reach of the file cabinet.

Take everything out of the file drawer and put it in a file box, hanging folders and all. Go through the box folder by folder and put back in the drawer only the files you know you'll need (probably 20 percent of the whole—research shows that we never use 80 percent of what we keep). Toss or recycle the rest, or transfer it to off-site storage if you need to keep it.

A FRESH START

To indicate large categories within your file drawer, use colored hanging folders or colored plastic index tabs. For example, project A would use red hanging folders, project B blue, and so on. As a general rule, use only one manila folder per hanging folder. When you're labeling folders, ask yourself: If I want this again, what word will I think of first? Your first answer is usually a good file title.

Organize your files alphabetically, chronologically, or whatever other way works for you. Just be consistent.

If you organize your files by major category, you'll find documents more quickly. At the same time, there's nothing wrong with creating a file for just one piece of paper if it will simplify retrieval—especially if it's something you use often.

A major reason why filing systems break down is that people forget exactly

Knowing where to find your files can help you save the day.

what they named a particular folder. Are those papers filed under "Car" or "Automobile" or "Vehicle"? A simple tool can fix that: a *file index,* a list of all the folders by name. (For a sample file index, see page 137.) Create your file index on your computer so you can update it quickly. (Handwrite changes on a printout between updates.) Keep one copy at your desk and post another on the filing cabinet so it's easily accessible.

Always check your file index before you label a new folder, to see if an appropriate file for a specific category already exists. That way, you'll avoid making a file for "Venues" when you already have one for "Meeting Locations."

Also, remember that the purpose of a filing system is not just to put papers away, but to be able to locate them again.

To facilitate the process, file information according to how you will use it, not where you got it. For instance, if you attended a management conference and received some handouts on interviewing techniques, file them under "Interviewing Techniques," not "Human Resources Seminar."

STORING DISKS

Keep computer disks that you use often on your desk, sorted by type—floppy disks, optical disks, CD-ROMs. Office-supply stores offer a variety of containers designed for these media. You can arrange disks by client, project, date, or file type, such as word processing.

If you have a disk for proposals and a disk for client X, where do you put a proposal you wrote for client X? One solution is to number each disk, then create a list

BUSINESS CARD SMARTS

INSTEAD OF TOSSING LOOSE BUSINESS CARDS into a drawer, keep them together in one place. You never know when you'll need the phone number for that consultant you met at last year's conference, or the e-mail address of your recruiter.

Simple Enter the information in your computerized contact manager program. You can also use a card scanner if your company has one. Putting the information on your computer makes it easy to search for a name.

Simpler Staple or tape the business cards directly onto rotary file cards that are at least as large. Another option is to buy stick-on fasteners or punches that allow you to insert the business cards directly into your file.

Simplest Empty a box of your own business cards and use it to file your contacts' business cards alphabetically—by name or business. Keep your own supply of business cards in your briefcase or purse.

in your computer that describes the contents of each disk. You can use the computer's search capability to quickly find whatever document you need.

MAKING IT EASY

One of the primary stumbling blocks to filing is overstuffed drawers. Make sure you don't pack the files so tightly you can't fit your hand inside. Leave at least three inches (8cm) of extra space. Also, if you use hanging file folders, attach the plastic tab to the front of the folder so that when you're ready to file you can grasp the tab and pull it forward, creating space for the newest piece of paper. As you handle an individual file, take an extra minute to purge it of old documents. Dating papers as you file them (putting the month and year in the upper right-hand corner) will help make this task easier.

If you have very thick files or if you want to put several manila files in one hanging folder, use accordion-type hanging files (for extra width) or use hanging files with pockets (for the small stuff).

Consider using a card file as a mini filing system for scraps of papers containing names, numbers, and other bits of vital information. Buy one in a size that's large enough to allow you to staple or tape business cards or sticky notes directly onto the cards. Get one without a lid so you won't be tempted to stack items on top instead of putting the information away immediately. Arrange the information in your card file according to what topic you would think of when you want to retrieve it. You may file your colleagues by last name, for instance, but the graphic artist whose name you can never remember should go under "Graphic Artists."

If you have business cards from several companies that offer the same product or similar services, put them together under a general topic ("Office Supplies") to make it easier to choose the best candidate for

As you handle a file, take an extra minute to purge it of old documents. Writing the date on papers as you file them will make this easier.

the job. You can also create cards that are cross-indexes of other cards in your file. For example, on a blank card headed "Painters" you might list "Acme Painting," "Bob's Painting Service," and "Painting Unlimited"—and add a note that their business cards are elsewhere in the file.

MAINTAINING SUCCESS

Just as that office aspidistra needs watering and trimming, your simplified filing system will need some attention to maintain its effectiveness. Judicious pruning from time to time keeps your filing system vigorous and sturdy.

Ask any group of people whether they have papers in their files they know they could throw out, and you'll always get some raised hands. Why don't they toss those useless papers? Often people feel guilty about cleaning out files because it isn't billable time. Consider this: It's good business to make information easy to find, because you'll ultimately save time. And your slimmer, trimmer filing system means that your company won't need to spend money to buy extra filing cabinets.

Maybe you aren't the one who has the final say on which files are thrown away and which ones are kept. If that's the case, use your file index to let the one in charge know which files you want to discard and why. Print a copy of the index and annotate it with notes such as "three years old" or "no longer accurate."

To be effective, your file index must be a living document, a mirror of your filing system. Add and delete file names as you add and delete actual files. Study your company's retention guidelines and any legal requirements so you know which records to keep and for how long.

Each time you file a new document, note the retention guideline on the label ("Keep for one year") for quick and easy upkeep. If you run out of file space, find a place to archive files you no longer use but need to keep for legal reasons. Discard them when enough time has elapsed.

Reviewing documents *and tossing outdated ones will keep your files free of clutter. It's easier to find a document quickly when there are fewer papers to search through.*

MAKING the MOST of
high-tech Tools

—✳—

1 Harness the power of the **computer** to make short work of creating, sharing, and updating business information. **2** Choose **software** with features that are appropriate to the tasks you perform most often. **3** Invest time in **training** to take full advantage of available technology. **4** Develop a workable system for **organizing** computer files so you can find items quickly and easily. **5** Set up and follow a program of **file backup,** virus protection, and hard-disk maintenance to avoid disaster. **6** Know and observe electronic etiquette in order to communicate effectively in cyberspace. **7** Get familiar with some **Internet** search engines to locate timely information. **8** Streamline your use of the telephone to make a good **impression** and get your job done more effectively. **9** Take advantage of **mobile** technology, such as cellular phones, pagers, and handheld computers, to stay in touch with customers and coworkers. **10** Turn off your cell phone when you're off duty to give yourself some **downtime.** ●

WORKING WITH TECHNOLOGY

SIMPLIFYING THE ELECTRONIC OFFICE

* —— * —— *

Love it or hate it (more likely both), technology is essential to the workplace. Used wisely, computers can enhance your workday by eliminating unnecessary duplication of effort, increasing productivity, and fostering better communication with your colleagues and your customers.

But don't get caught up in feeling that you need every new gizmo or the latest versions of your software. If you install only the programs you use frequently (or those your company requires) and learn them well, chances are you can take better advantage of the system you already have.

Similarly, keeping abreast of portable technology, e-mail, and the Internet can give you a leg up, but be sure your excursions in cyberspace are saving time and not wasting it.

Technical proficiency can make an employee stand out in the workplace, so improving your skills may not only ease your current job—it may help you get a better one.

Being a Savvy Computer User

✳

THERE'S NO DOUBT THAT COMPUTERS CAN SAVE TIME. WITH SPREADSHEETS YOU CAN INSTANTLY PERFORM CALCULATIONS, JUST AS QUICKLY TRANSLATE RESULTS INTO PIE CHARTS, THEN PASTE THEM INTO A PRESENTATION PACKAGE.

Word processors have transformed the laborious process of typing, revising, correcting, and retyping. Databases store vast amounts of information and assemble it in a variety of useful and imaginative ways. Presentation software lets you quickly create a slide presentation and instant handouts, while a desktop publishing program can create a professional-quality document in hours. Project management software helps you track tasks, dates, and responsibilities, and scheduling software helps you coordinate the efforts of your team.

With all these tools, the challenge is to use them effectively so they save time,

not waste it. If you're creating just a single report, for instance, it doesn't make sense to spend an hour or more setting up complicated style sheets. But if you have to generate a similar report frequently, or if you need to customize that report for 12 different departments, taking the time to automate formatting can pay off.

THE RIGHT TOOL

To streamline your work and minimize frustration, use the right software for the job rather than coax a program into doing something it wasn't designed for. On the other hand, don't use so many different

Avoid unnecessary bells and whistles; stick to what you need in a computer.

programs that you can't master any of them. Recognize when you need a specialized program and when you don't.

If, for example, you're inserting a few simple graphics on your page and formatting one or two blocks of text, your word processor will probably be fine. But if you require precise placement of a complex banner and fancy typography, you'll do better with a desktop publishing program. There are several such programs available. Choose one that is relatively simple, such as Microsoft Publisher, unless you plan to use it every day. High-end design software, such as QuarkXPress or Adobe PageMaker, is so sophisticated that only professional graphic artists use the majority of these programs' many features.

To decide which tools are best, solicit advice from people inside and outside your company who are experienced with the kinds of tasks you need to perform. You may discover that the software you have is perfectly adequate, even if there's a newer version on the market. If you decide that your job requires specialized or upgraded software, ask your company for these tools. You'll be more successful in your requests if you give solid examples of how the purchase will save money and time.

TIME SAVERS

You'll know you need better tools when you find yourself repeating the same task over and over or when you lose track of the many facets of your job. If the challenge is, say, managing your to-do list, a personal information manager such as Day-Timer Organizer will automate your calendar and

Faster Formatting

The report generators that come with many databases and contact managers are difficult and time consuming to learn. Unless you create complicated reports frequently, it's usually faster to import the data into a word-processing file. Then use your word processor's more familiar tools to arrange the data in the format you need.

your schedule. If you need to juggle others' schedules as well as your own, consider a scheduling program. It can save hours of phone tag if you're the one responsible for setting up meetings. Schedulers can find blocks of time when everyone is available and notify each person by e-mail.

A fax-modem for your computer can be another big time saver. It can look up a number in its address list, dial the recipient's fax machine, and fax a document directly from your computer (no printing required). If your fax doesn't go through, the fax-modem automatically redials. Also, if you don't want to tie up your line, you can instruct it to send faxes during lunch or at night. On the other hand, receiving incoming faxes with a computer can be a nuisance if there's just one phone line at your desk or if you don't keep your computer on 24 hours a day.

Remember, though, that the best tools for you may be pen and paper: If your job calls for just a few appointments a week, it's easier to jot them down on a calendar than to master an automated scheduler.

SOFTWARE SHORTCUTS

The beauty of having information in electronic form is that you never have to type it again. You can reuse it for whatever you need. It's easy to cut and paste within a file, between files in the same program, or even between programs. It all works the same way: Highlight the information you want, cut or copy it, move your cursor to where you want it to appear, and paste.

It's sometimes faster to update an old document, especially a complex one, since you may lose formatting on pieces of information that you cut and paste. Just save the old document under a new name, then revise it with new data as needed.

Styles—preset formats that you apply to text—can also save time. You can apply a style to text (for example, a format for headings) with just one or two mouse clicks. Not only does this speed things up, it ensures consistency in your document. And if you decide you don't like the look of, say, your photo captions, you simply change the applicable style.

Set up any frequently used boilerplate text so it's ready to insert into a document with just a few keystrokes. There are different ways to do this. AutoFill in Microsoft

> **There's no point in learning about features you don't need; the trick is to focus your efforts.**

Excel automatically enters text into a spreadsheet. In Microsoft Word, Auto-Correct or AutoText replaces portions of your text with whatever you specify. For example, you can type in your initials and have the program replace them with your name. Find and Replace can accomplish the same task. Instead of typing "Santa Fe, New Mexico" repeatedly (and possibly introducing errors), type "SF," then search for and replace them all.

Find and Replace is also handy for catching typos that your spelling check may miss. For example, suppose you type "form" when you mean "from." The software sees this as a correctly spelled word and ignores it. But you can search for all instances of "form" and change them to "from" where it's appropriate.

You might also consider working with templates—documents that have formatting, and perhaps some text, ready to go.

Content First, Format Last

Although visual impressions are important, content is even more crucial. Finish writing the content first, then use any time left to format the information. That way you'll be sure to complete the most important aspect of the report, and you won't waste time formatting something you decide to change later.

For example, you could create a template for the standard letter you send to all new clients. Each time you get new clients, just add the appropriate names and addresses (or better yet, merge them from your database) to create introductory letters.

A LITTLE LEARNING

Without question, one of the best investments you can make in simplifying your workday (and advancing your career) is computer training. Research shows that the typical user takes advantage of less than 20 percent of the capabilities of the software he or she uses. It's worth delving into the advanced features of applications you use regularly. These can speed your work and make it look more polished.

Obviously, there's no point in learning about features you don't need; the trick is to look at the challenges you face and see how your computer can help. Spend some time analyzing the kinds of work you do (or want to do). Then choose one or two areas in which you can focus your efforts. If you need to learn the basic operating system such as Windows or Macintosh, train on this first—it's a good investment of your time. Then move on to the individual programs you use.

To make learning your computer programs easier, first familiarize yourself with the logic of their menu systems. That way when you need a certain feature, you'll have a better idea where to find it. Glance at all the choices each time you pull down a menu. Even if something doesn't make sense at first, you may realize what a particular option refers to when the need arises.

Learning advanced *features of the software you use regularly will help you streamline your efforts and work more quickly.*

You can also skim the manual, or at least read the table of contents, to see what features you might have a use for. And these days different programs function similarly enough that mastering one program makes it quicker and easier to learn others.

When you're trying out new features, you'll probably make errors. Usually the Undo button on the program's toolbar or the Undo command in the Edit menu will repair any damage. It's also a good idea to save your file before you try a new feature. If you mess up your file beyond repair, just close it without saving. When you reopen the file, it will be exactly the same as it was before the experiment.

TRACKING FILES

There are several ways to organize your files on your hard disk or network drive. Both your office policies and your personal preferences will determine your choice.

Many software programs are set up to save the files you create in the program's

---　✳︎　---

individual folder. However, this method leaves your files scattered all over your hard disk and makes it difficult to back them up—so change your software's default settings. Other programs save your files in one main folder. Although this is a slightly better method, you can modify it to work even more effectively. One way is to create subfolders within your main folder that refer to work categories. You might have categories like correspondence, reports, newsletters, finances, and personnel matters. Or you could have categories that refer to your different clients.

Some people prefer to have subfolder categories that refer to software types (word processing, spreadsheet, and so on), but as software becomes more sophisticated these distinctions are less important.

When you create files, keep the organizing system in mind. Add the category into the file name; for example, end it with *ltr* or *budget*. That way you can use the Find File command in the operating system or the File Open command of many programs to find all files of that type, regardless of what folders they're in.

A second option is to use one main folder (such as My Documents) for all the data you create, and then type in extended names to describe the files. With the long file names possible on all Macintosh and newer Windows computers, you can pack in plenty of helpful information.

For example, the file name of a report you wrote could include the title, the client's name, and the publication name, date, and editor (for example, Interviewing Strategies—XYZ Corporation, XYZ Publication, 09.01.98, Sally Brown). Using the Find File feature, you'll be able to find that file quickly by searching for any word in the title. If you do a search for the words *XYZ Corporation* you'll find all the files you created for that client.

SAFEGUARDING DATA

One sure way to reduce stress in your life is to be prepared for disaster. These strategies will help stave off the unthinkable: losing a file when you need it urgently.

Back up your work. It's essential to do this regularly in case your hard disk is damaged, the network goes down, or you lose power. For critical files, make backups throughout the day. Even if you store files on a network that's backed up daily, keep a spare copy of crucial files. It could take a day or more to restart a crashed network.

Guard against power loss. Protect all your expensive equipment from voltage damage by plugging it into a surge suppressor. There are surge suppressors for your modem's phone line, too. Consider an uninterruptible power supply (UPS).

If the power fails, its battery can keep your computer running long enough for you to save what you're working on and shut down your computer properly to avoid damage. It has built-in surge suppression.

Watch out for viruses. If you use the Internet or share disks with other people, it's only a matter of time before you get a virus, so use virus-protection software to minimize your risk. Keep this software current (new viruses are created all the time) by getting regular updates directly from the vendor's Web site.

Tidy up. To keep your hard disk operating at its best (and to identify potential problems), use disk scanning and defragmenting utilities. Have your technical support person (or an unofficial guru) show you how to do this, or do it for you.

An office computer network *with a backup system will help save important documents even if individual workstations break down.*

Surviving in Cyberspace

——— ✳ ———

WE'RE LIVING AND WORKING IN AN AGE OF INSTANT COMMUNICATION—
E-MAIL AND THE INTERNET'S WORLD WIDE WEB HAVE REVOLUTIONIZED
THE WAY WE SEND AND RECEIVE INFORMATION EACH DAY.

Along with increased speed and convenience of information, however, has come vastly increased volume. But you needn't be overwhelmed—the trick is to learn a few effective strategies for coping with it.

When you need to exchange detailed information fast, nothing beats e-mail. In fact, it's so convenient that people often get hundreds of e-mail messages a day. So if you want them to read yours, use clear, specific subject lines. Sometimes you can convey the entire message in the subject line. Keep your e-mail short and to the point. If a long message is essential, summarize the content at the beginning.

Think Before You Send

To guard against the embarrassment of accidentally sending a message before you've made sure it's worded the way you want (especially if the e-mail is going to a customer), leave the address line blank until you're all done. This also helps guard against sending a message to the wrong person.

E-mail might be faster than regular mail, but it is best not used for time-sensitive messages, as there's no guarantee they'll be read soon enough. Many intraoffice networks have an Urgent option for flagging time-critical e-mail; but if you overuse it, your words may be ignored. Another option is Receipt Requested, which notifies you that the addressee has received (but not necessarily read) your message. Sometimes the recipient will be informed that a receipt is being sent, too, so don't abuse this feature: Some people may feel that you're checking up on them.

Although e-mail programs make it easy to send a copy of your message to lots of people, resist the temptation. Why torment your coworkers with unnecessary information? If you restrain yourself, your colleagues might get the idea and resist copying you on everything, too.

Whenever you send a message, think of it as a postcard: You have no control over who sees it. If you erase the message on your system, your recipient may still keep it—or forward it to someone else in the office. Even if both of you delete the message, it could remain on the network backup, and other people in the company might be able to access it.

Also, chances are good your employer has the right to monitor your e-mail, just

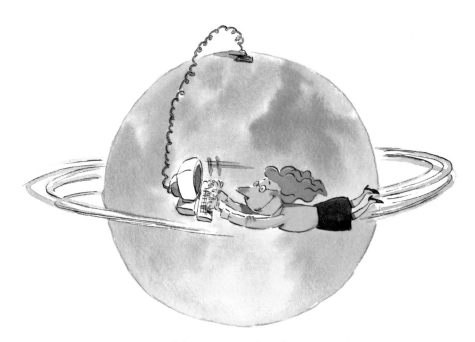

E-mail lets you conduct business at lightning speed with all parts of the globe.

as he or she does your phone calls. And if you're ever involved in a lawsuit, all paper and electronic records can be subpoenaed. So never state anything electronically that you wouldn't want to say to the recipient's face—or see in the morning newspaper. If you're feeling angry or upset, you should

have it automatically delete messages that are recognizable as junk e-mail. Unfortunately, not all programs have filters. Check with your system administrator, or if you don't have one, look in the program manual to see if you can set this up for yourself. If you don't have a filter, your e-mail

You have no control over who sees your e-mail messages. Never state anything electronically that you wouldn't want to see in the newspaper.

probably sleep on it before you fire off a message. Remember also that the recipient cannot hear your tone of voice, so he or she may misinterpret your message if you're writing with tongue in cheek.

STEMMING THE TIDE

One way to manage the flood of incoming e-mail is to filter your messages. For example, your mail program could notify you when you get a message from your boss or an important client. Or, you can

system may let you sort messages by subject or sender so that you can filter out the junk e-mail quickly.

Store the messages you keep in separate folders for each project or for each person you communicate with regularly. This will vastly simplify the task of finding a particular message when you want to review it. (As you search for messages, you'll notice how helpful it is when the subject header describes the contents, so keep those subject lines informative.)

Send a Hard Copy

E-mail is an excellent method for exchanging ideas, information, and drafts. However, it's not advisable for closing a deal or drawing up a final contract: Electronic documents are too easy to alter after the fact. Always follow up an important e-mail exchange with a hard copy summarizing talks you've had and agreements you've reached.

Unless your company or your personal needs dictate otherwise, choose one or two blocks of time during the day to read your e-mail. This is much more efficient

The Internet *makes it easier to do your work from any location and to connect with a far-flung network of colleagues.*

than checking messages throughout the day. The time you lose getting back on track after each interruption may seem negligible, but it adds up. If you can give a response quickly—such as confirming you'll be at a meeting—do it. (When replying to e-mail, be sure to quote all or part of the original message in case the writer doesn't remember it.) Likewise, if you need to make a quick note on your calendar, take care of that immediately. Then you can delete the message.

You can handle messages that require follow-up in two ways: Print them all and add them to your paper action-file system, or move them into a to-do e-mail folder on your computer. Be sure to check this folder daily so you'll be up to date.

If your system administrator doesn't have a set schedule for deleting e-mail messages, devise a simple system for your own use. Old messages can fill your hard drive and, depending on how your software works, slow down your system. So make

"housekeeping" a regular chore, perhaps every two weeks. Delete unimportant messages and save anything vital to a separate disk. You may be able to set your e-mail system to delete messages after a certain interval—just be sure you save important messages before the system erases them.

WELCOME TO THE WEB

Massive amounts of information are at your fingertips with the Internet. You can gather the latest information about a company with whom you are doing business; learn more about a competitor; find a new supplier; make airline, hotel, and car reservations; download road maps and driving instructions; or even order food for the office. Or you can stay abreast of developments in your field, find a job, or monitor your retirement portfolio. You can also solicit ideas from colleagues through newsgroups that concern your profession.

There's lots of fluff on the Internet, though, so be prepared to wade through it or find shortcuts around it. Experiment with the different ways to search. Search engines like Yahoo and Lycos categorize sites by subject and also let you search by keyword: Type in a word and they list the Web pages containing it. Some sites send keywords to numerous search engines.

Since all search engines work a little differently, you might want to try identical searches on a number of them until you see which ones usually give the best results. Then learn to use those two or three really well. For all search engines, you'll get better results if you use multiword searches, such as the name of the

Smart Searching

When you enter two or more words in an Internet search field, the search engine will find sites that contain any of the words. If you want to find sites that contain all the words, put a plus sign (+) in front of each of them. If you're looking for words in a certain order, such as the phrase "profit and loss statement," put it inside quotes.

product and the company instead of just the product. Look for a button that says Advanced, Options, Tips, Help, or something similar to refine your searches.

When you're learning to use the Internet, take it in bite-size pieces. Start with a search in an area that interests you professionally—or one you pursue as a hobby, since your enjoyment will motivate you to keep going past the frustrations.

Before you go online, have a clear goal in mind and stay focused on it. You can easily spend hours clicking on links and never find the information you need. If you see sites that interest you, bookmark them for a later session. It's easier to resist checking out a site if you know you can get back to it later. You might also keep a paper file where you note the addresses of interesting sites. Then, once a week or so, designate a time to browse the Web, starting with the bookmarks you made earlier. Delete those that don't pan out.

REACH OUT AND
TOUCH SOMEONE

———— ✳ ————

INCREASINGLY, COMPANIES EXPECT THEIR EMPLOYEES TO STAY IN TOUCH BY CARRYING PAGERS AND CELL PHONES. YOUR ABILITY TO REACH OTHERS— OR TO BE REACHED—CAN LEAD TO BETTER WORK WITH LESS EFFORT.

The telephone has been around for more than a century, but it's still unsurpassed as a timesaving business tool. It offers the unparalleled convenience of holding a dialogue, in real time, with someone in the next office building or on the other side of the world. Used properly, this truly amazing device can help you make decisions, reach conclusions, minimize misunderstandings, and close deals. Used improperly, the telephone can be a major waste of your precious time.

Give Yourself a Call

If you're out of the office and suddenly you remember a task you need to perform or a meeting you should attend, call yourself and leave a voice mail message. Many voice mail systems have an option that lets you postpone delivery of a message so that it arrives at a certain time—such as just before you need to take care of the task or leave your office for the meeting.

Research indicates that an average business phone call lasts 18 minutes, but with preparation it might take place in a third less time. If you made 10 calls a day, that would translate to a potential savings of one precious hour. How do you shave time off your calls? It's really quite simple. Before you dial, take a minute to prepare.

PHONE ETIQUETTE

Proper phone etiquette is key whether you are initiating a call or receiving it. Here are a few tips designed to streamline your business calls and ensure that the telephone remains an effective tool for you.

Set a time. Reserve an hour or so each day to initiate and return calls.

Have your paperwork at hand. This might mean getting additional information about the person you're calling, such as the name of an assistant who might answer, or where you met or last talked to this person. (You can use your database or personal information manager to store and retrieve this kind of information.)

Prepare an agenda. When you have several unrelated topics to discuss, making a list with bullet points will help you remember each one. If you have only a minute to talk, you can cover the most important points. If you have more time, you'll be sure not to miss anything, and you'll avoid the embarrassment of having to call right back with, "I forgot to ask…" If you have to leave a message, you'll do so more succinctly and professionally.

Call at the right time. Ask people you call if this is a good time to talk. If it's not, arrange a convenient time to call back.

State your purpose. At the start of the call, always identify yourself and the reason you're calling. It sounds professional and it gets right to the point.

Answer the phone assertively. A pleasant "How can I help you?" or "What can I do for you?" moves the conversation forward.

State a time frame for the call. Say, for example, "I can talk for 10 minutes," and outline the points you need to discuss. Then, stick to your time frame.

Save time for your callers. When you set up your voice mail system or answering machine, make your greeting message as succinct as possible, while keeping it friendly. Avoid trite phrases like "Your call

"You're It!"

You can minimize telephone tag by suggesting several callback times, another phone number, or other ways that you can be reached, such as through e-mail or a paging system. Always leave your phone number, in case the person you're calling is picking up messages from outside the office and hasn't brought along your telephone number.

is important to us." If you have to leave a long greeting with many options, provide an escape hatch that tells callers how to reach a live person or skip your message.

MANAGING CONTACTS

If your job requires you to keep in touch with dozens of people on a regular basis, you might want to think about contact

Good phone manners help you connect with your clients.

Laptop or PDA?

If you travel and you use your computer primarily to write reports or crunch numbers, you probably need a laptop with a full-size keyboard and at least a 10-inch (25cm) display. If you use your computer mainly to retrieve schedules, phone numbers, or faxes, you might be a candidate for a pocket-size PDA (personal digital assistant).

management software. Contact managers keep track of all your clients and coworkers, including not only their names, addresses, and phone numbers, but also the product they buy or sell, their locations, areas of specialty, and so on. With a contact manager, you can search your contacts using any combination of these subjects. You can find all your clients who have fire

> **The quest for speed and convenience has spawned an entire industry of communication gadgets that integrate voice, data, and faxing.**

insurance within a certain geographical area, for example, or all the customers who bought phones during May.

Most contact management products also schedule appointments and help you plan a sales strategy. Some have templates for specific industries such as real estate

and insurance. If you're on the road a lot, a contact manager is probably your best bet. Contact managers are more difficult to learn than personal information managers, but they offer a much more powerful database and search engine.

GOING MOBILE

Not too many years ago, cellular phones and pagers were used only in life-or-death situations. But as the technology has improved and prices have fallen, these devices have become routine business tools that dramatically increase your ability to stay in touch with the public. In fact, it has become vital in many industries to provide 24-hour access for clients in order to improve customer service and accommodate people in different time zones.

The quest for speed and convenience has spawned an entire industry of multifunction communication gadgets that integrate voice, data, and fax messaging, and may well incorporate a Web browser, complete with screen and keyboard. Some are designed to work with Personal Communication Services (PCSs)—new digital networks that operate at a frequency different from that of cellular networks. These services often offer a more competitive rate than the cellular companies do. But prices and support vary among providers, so it's a smart idea to shop around.

The ability to plug into your desktop from afar can be a godsend. If you spend a lot of time away from your office and your data is confined to your desktop computer, all the customer information, appointments, and tasks you've entered are not of much use. What are you going to do when you're marooned in an airport and an important client expects an immediate response to her urgent request?

One solution is to always carry a notebook computer or a laptop. But a range of handheld computing devices, or personal digital assistants (PDAs), can do this job more easily. Many of these devices come with miniature versions of a word processor, spreadsheet, and database; a calendar; an e-mail program; and a Web browser. Some PDAs use a small keyboard, while others combine a stylus and handwriting recognition technology.

You can synchronize PDAs with the computer at your office, meaning that you can fetch data from your computer into your handheld device, make changes, and transfer the data back to your computer. Not all handhelds have this capability, so be sure you know exactly what you need when you're purchasing a PDA.

CELLULAR BURNOUT

As convenient as these tools are, beware of the downside to portable technology. Psychologists report seeing increasing numbers of "wired" patients who complain about feeling stressed but don't see the connection between burnout and having a cell phone as a constant companion. All of the stress-reduction exercises in the world will not compensate for a workday run by gimmicks, gadgets, and gizmos that create more problems for you than they solve. Figure out which of these devices you really need, and then set limits on the amount of time you use them.

IF YOUR JOB REQUIRES THAT YOU KEEP IN TOUCH WITH MORE PEOPLE THAN YOU CAN COUNT, THESE TOOLS WILL HELP.

◈

Business card organizer
If you use a handful of business cards regularly, a binder that keeps the cards visible in plastic sleeves is probably your best tool.

Business card scanner
If you collect business cards on a daily basis, a business card scanner can help you put them to work. The scanner will enter information on the cards into a computer, where you can store it in a database.

Personal digital assistant
A PDA can link you to your office computer while you're on the road. Most PDAs offer a database and spreadsheet, and some can retrieve e-mail or voice mail.

Contact management software
Applications in this category let you maintain a database of customers or colleagues. They can search for names, dates, products, or any other information you enter.

Rotary card file
The dependable card file sometimes works better than any gizmo on the market. You can attach adhesive strips to business cards and file them there for easy, quick retrieval.

TOOLS for STRESS
Management

—✳—

1 Take care of your physical and emotional **well-being** with healthful eating, exercise, and time with family and friends. **2** Deal positively with a difficult **coworker** to maintain a cooperative, supportive workplace and to accomplish your goals. **3** Prepare for your next **presentation,** whether before a crowd or across the desk, and wow your audience. **4** Approach your performance **review** as an opportunity to outline your accomplishments and glean ideas for improving your work skills. **5** To simplify business **travel,** keep an updated checklist to remind you to pack everything you need. **6** While on the **road,** act promptly on any papers you receive so you'll have less work when you return. **7** Don't be afraid to **change jobs** if you're dissatisfied with your present situation. Schedule informational interviews so you can get acquainted with potential employers. **8** Do your homework and hone your **interview** skills to get the job you really want. **9** Remember that finding a good job takes **time** and effort. ●

COPING WITH STRESS

STAYING CALM WHEN THE PRESSURE IS ON

✳ —— ✳ —— ✳

Let's face it: If you work, you are going to experience stress. Depending on your personality and mind-set, any of the myriad difficulties that crop up on the job could make you feel pressured—too much (or even too little) work to do, changes in procedures and policies, a lack of relevant information, unclear expectations from your boss, tasks that are beyond your abilities, or unrealistic deadlines. Disruptions that can really send anxiety levels soaring include business travel and—the ultimate stressor—looking for a new job.

Our bodies respond to stressful circumstances with the ancient fight-or-flight defense, which pumps out hormones, speeds up the heart rate, and increases blood flow to the brain. If they persist, such biological changes can be debilitating. On the other hand, occasional stress stimulates us both biologically and intellectually, giving us an edge. The key is to keep stress from taking over your workday.

MANAGING
EVERYDAY STRESS

———— ✳ ————

D O ANY OF THESE SOUND FAMILIAR? YOUR COMPUTER CRASHES AT 2 P.M. THE
DAY BEFORE THE JONES PROPOSAL IS DUE. THE TEAM LEADER HAS THE FLU,
AND YOU HAVE TO GIVE A PRESENTATION TO THE GROUP IN HER PLACE.

And, the only administrative assistant in your office has just handed in a resignation letter. When you're faced with crises like these, you may feel that your next important decision is whether to take an antacid tablet or have a good cry. But some simple strategies will increase your ability to handle stress and turn negative circumstances into positive results.

The first step is to get in shape physically. You can't hope to put forth your best effort unless you're feeling good. It's no accident that the corporate world is increasing employees' access to fitness facilities (either on- or off-site). Exercise can relieve stress and provide tangible health benefits. Furthermore, regular aerobic exercise enhances your energy, your mood, and your productivity—not to mention your ability to cope. So join that lunchtime power-walking group or make time for that racquetball game.

Don't underestimate the importance of getting enough sleep. Research shows that sleeping does more than rejuvenate our bodies. It also helps our brains process information more effectively. Next time

A brisk walk *at noontime or on your way to work can help you feel more energetic during the day. Keep workout clothes in your office so you'll have no excuse not to exercise.*

you're struggling with a complex problem, you might hit on the solution more easily if you go to bed early the night before.

Another easy stress buster is to drink at least four glasses of water during the day. Avoid coffee or caffeinated drinks, because they act as diuretics and actually increase fluid needs. Dehydration reduces blood flow to the brain, decreasing efficiency and producing a feeling of exhaustion.

Research suggests that food can affect your mental state, too. Carbohydrates tend to calm you down, while meals high in protein can aid reaction time and mental acuity. Sweets or chocolate make you feel more energetic in the short term, but your body reacts by releasing excessive amounts of insulin, which causes a serious energy dip shortly after the sugar high. The volume of food you eat affects your mental state as well. For example, gorging on a huge meal right before you head into a meeting could leave you nodding off at the conference table before long.

Another major factor in handling stress is your attitude toward yourself and the situation. Shed these unrealistic attitudes that set you up for failure:

◆ NEEDING UNANIMOUS APPROVAL

◆ BELIEVING EVENTS SHOULD TURN OUT THE WAY YOU WANT THEM TO

◆ THINKING PEOPLE SHOULD ALWAYS RESPOND THE WAY YOU EXPECT

◆ EXPECTING TO WIN ALL THE TIME

◆ BELIEVING PAST BAD EXPERIENCES WILL DETERMINE FUTURE RESULTS

Finally, your network of friends and family are among your best weapons against stress. Schedule recreation time in your planner rather than waiting for opportunities to come up spontaneously. Stay connected with people you care about to rejuvenate your mind, body, and spirit.

PROBLEM COWORKERS

Just about any workplace has someone with whom it's difficult to work. Often the best strategy is not to take the offending behavior personally. That's easier said than done, of course, but well worth the effort if it means reducing your stress. Do the very best job you can and let go of the rest. With practice, you *can* learn to be diplomatic with difficult people.

Talk directly to the troublesome colleague. Although confrontation is difficult, it may be the only way to clarify the issues.

But if someone else's actions—or non-actions—are preventing you from doing your job, you'll have to remedy the problem. Talking directly to the troublesome colleague is often the most effective solution. Although confrontation is difficult, it may be the only way to clarify the issues. Otherwise, you can get caught up in a pattern of silent resentment or nervously trying to guess someone's reaction, both of which drain your energy. (See pages 54–56 for advice on resolving conflicts.)

Sometimes talking it out doesn't work. You've said what there is to say, maybe more than once, but the behavior doesn't change. The problem may be one of differing work styles or perhaps even rivalry.

It's time to speak to your supervisor. First, though, make a list of the specific negative results caused by your colleague's behavior. For example, "I had to leave my desk six times in one day to answer the front desk phone because no one was there," or, "We've had four complaints this week from customers who received the wrong order." Then meet with your boss and present the facts calmly.

There are some stressors you should never ignore. Do not tolerate any sexual harassment or any type of discrimination by either your boss or a coworker. Remember that sexual harassment includes not only unwanted sexual advances but also jokes, stories, pictures, or objects that are offensive, alarming, annoying, abusive, or demeaning. Workplace discrimination may be based on age, sex, religion, race, sexual orientation, or physical handicap. Be aware of your company's policies regarding these issues as well as applicable federal and state laws. You should immediately report harassment or discrimination to a supervisor in writing.

STAGE FRIGHT

The Book of Lists ranks public speaking as the most common phobia. In fact, some people claim they would rather eat live spiders than speak publicly. Why is being in the spotlight so terrifying? People often fear that they'll open their mouths and nothing will come out. Or that even if they do manage to spit out the right words, their message will bomb—that no one will be entertained or enlightened, much less

Win over your audience by making your presentation lively.

persuaded of the speaker's point of view. Not to worry—a few simple strategies will ensure your success.

As you write your speech, concentrate on preparing a strong opening and closing. One simple method of engaging an audience at the beginning is to ask a question: "Did you know…?" or "Have you ever…?" Close with a simple recap of the main points of your presentation and

To minimize the jitters, practice your talk, timing yourself as you go. Run through it several times using note cards to guide you.

include a call to action, such as a challenge for members of the sales force to bring in two new accounts each.

Consider using presentation tools to create additional interest. Given your subject, audience, and material, what would be appropriate and effective? A monthly sales report to your team might need nothing more than a flip chart, a whiteboard, or a handout. For a sales pitch to an important client or a speech at an association meeting, a series of overheads can provide more polish. Software such as Microsoft PowerPoint can incorporate audio and video clips, graphics, and simple special effects. If you need something fancier, a multimedia service can create a sophisticated presentation for you.

To minimize the jitters, practice your talk, timing yourself as you go along. Run through the speech several times using note cards or a printout of your overheads

GIVING A TALK IS LESS STRESSFUL WHEN YOU HAVE GOOD PROPS. THESE PORTABLE TOOLS WILL HELP YOU MAKE YOUR CASE.

◈

Light box
Use a portable light box (top) to show transparencies up to 9 by 12 inches (23cm by 30cm) in size. Or use it to display slides if you're working with a few people at a table. The device folds up to fit inside a briefcase.

Poster tube
This rigid plastic tube lets you roll up poster-size materials—charts, maps, blueprints—so you can carry them compactly without wrinkling or creasing. A shoulder strap makes it easy to tote when your hands are full.

Binder
A binder will keep your transparencies, photographs, or charts organized and easy to find. If you give the same talk often, simply store the materials in the binder in the order in which you use them for your talk.

Laser pointers
If you're using a large wall chart or slides with your presentation, these pocket-size devices will help you point out each item in your discussion. They emit a narrow laser beam that can pinpoint a spot across even a large room.

Give It the Once-Over

Arrive early for any presentation to be certain the room is set up correctly, all the equipment is in place, handouts are collated, and so on. It could really throw you off track to end up at the wrong meeting room or find out at the last minute that the overhead projector has a burned-out bulb.

or computer presentation to guide you. The best professionals frequently practice in front of a mirror or use a video camera to hone their performance and appearance. When the big moment arrives, take a few

refer to will give you a sense of security and something to do with your hands. Or divert attention from yourself by turning down the lights and using a slide projector.

Establishing a relationship with your audience—one person at a time—is an easy way to reduce your stress. If possible, mingle with the group prior to your presentation. Then it will be easier to begin your talk by making eye contact with one friendly face, lingering just a moment to make a solid connection. Move on around the room to connect with another face, and another. Don't spend too much time fretting about a seemingly uninterested audience member. An inattentive listener may just have had a sleepless night or be brooding over an unrelated disagreement.

Harness your nervous energy to show enthusiasm for your subject. Smile! Your voice will sound better, and people will be

It's tough to accept criticism. Try to think of a critique as a job tune-up. End with a plan for improvement and a timeline for accomplishing it.

slow, deep breaths while you're waiting to begin. It will automatically relax you. Another effective strategy is to press your thumb against your forefinger—this will release nervous energy so you don't wind up tapping your fingers on the podium or jangling change in your pocket.

If you're standing in front of your audience rather than sitting at a conference table, you can release nervous energy unobtrusively by moving around. For instance, you might deliver your opener, then walk over to the flip chart to talk about it. Having something to point at or

more relaxed listening to you. (If you're delivering bad news, of course, a smile is inappropriate; acknowledge that what you are saying may be difficult for the audience.) Most of all, keep in mind that you were asked to present your ideas because someone valued what you had to say.

JOB REVIEWS

Although they're a wonderful opportunity to get constructive feedback, performance reviews can feel a bit like being graded in school. And if your next salary increase is riding on your appraisal, it's *really* a big deal. Remember that your review is an opportunity to present your case and toot your own horn, so gather up all the evidence you can to demonstrate your excellent work. Be fully prepared to explain how you think you are doing. It helps to take along a list of your accomplishments.

Your supervisor will likely come prepared with specific feedback about your performance—the good and the bad. You will probably enjoy hearing the good—so drink it in and feel encouraged. But what about the not-so-good? It's tough to accept criticism, even when it's presented with care and consideration. Try to think of a critique as a job tune-up, a chance to find out what is squeaking and needs a little lubrication. If your supervisor feels specific changes are needed, a good review will end with a plan for improvement and a timeline for accomplishing it.

Sometimes you feel that you've done a great job, but your boss doesn't think so. Situations like this might mean that you lacked a clear idea of what was expected of you. Maybe you were concentrating on getting the best price for some new equipment, so you waited to get quotes from 10 vendors before submitting your recommendation. It turned out that getting the equipment as soon as possible was a bigger priority than saving money. To avoid misunderstandings like this, ask for more precise instructions the next time.

A bad review might also be an indication that your job is not the right fit. You and your boss may have a personality clash, office politics may be working against you, or your job skills may be better suited in another field. As bitter a pill as it is to swallow, try to take the attitude that your supervisor is doing you a favor by letting you know it's time to move on. (Refer to page 112 for tips on job hunting.)

GIVING THE REVIEW

Appraising an employee's performance can be stressful, too. You want to motivate subordinates to do their best, but too much criticism may backfire, leading to a resignation or a drop in productivity. Your attitude will make a genuine difference in the outcome. Always begin with what the employee has done well. Ask what she feels good about, or what she thinks needs improvement. Also ask what you can do to help her perform her work better. Finally, give the employee a chance to react and make any additional comments. Follow up with a written record of all agreements and details of any required action plans.

Calm on the Outside

When you're in a performance review or giving a presentation, remember that you're nervous only on the inside. Your heart may be racing and your palms sweaty, but it's likely that you appear cool and collected. Don't apologize for being nervous— you'll only draw attention to it. Just move ahead and impress everyone with your calm manner.

WHEN THE SHOW'S ON THE ROAD

---※---

ALTHOUGH GETTING AWAY FROM THE OFFICE MAY SOUND LIKE A VACATION, BUSINESS TRAVEL IS NO PICNIC. IT OFTEN MEANS EATING AIRPORT FOOD, LIVING OUT OF A SUITCASE, AND JUGGLING A HECTIC SCHEDULE.

But the inconveniences are well worth it. The chance to attend a convention or meet a client or colleague face-to-face can really pay off for your career, as well as give you perspective on life in general. Unusual insights, creative ideas, invigorating discussions, and reflective solitude may all occur on the road if you let them.

Wise planning helps your trip go more smoothly, but recognize that you can't control everything. Try to go with the flow and keep an open mind. Losing your temper over a canceled flight won't get you to your meeting any earlier—just

grumpier. If you anticipate these kinds of catastrophes you'll be in a better position to cope if and when they happen.

Prepare for your trip well before you leave. Schedule appointments carefully. Be sure to allow enough travel time between each appointment in case your flight is late or you miss a train, and always get good directions. (Even when you're taking a cab, it helps to know where you're headed.) Consider eliminating the hassle of navigating in a strange place by booking a limo or getting a daily rate from a taxi company rather than renting a car.

Keep in touch even while you're traveling—clients will appreciate your quick responses.

For frequent travelers, a checklist of every conceivable item you'll need on a trip is a must. Using such a checklist is much simpler than reinventing the wheel each time. (See the sample list on page 139.) Add items to the list as they come up. Pack lightly, sticking to one color scheme and taking along easy-care clothes you can mix and match. Many seasoned travelers keep a prepacked toiletry and overnight kit ready to go at a moment's notice.

EASING THE TRIP

While some business travelers insist on carrying all their luggage onto the plane for a quick getaway, others find this only makes the trip more wearisome. If you check your baggage, you can use the time while you're waiting to claim it to make a few phone calls, prepare for your next appointment, or read some material you brought along. Just in case your luggage gets lost in transit, always travel in something you could wear for business, or take a suitable outfit with you in a carry-on bag.

When making travel reservations, be sure to state your preferences—vegetarian food, a nonsmoking room, a midsize car, and so on. If you usually travel on one airline, consider a membership in its frequent flier club so you can rack up free miles. For an additional fee, you may also want to join the airline's airport club so you'll have a comfortable place to meet and work at the airport. Also, having a club membership with a car rental agency will eliminate standing in line at the counter, and frequently the agency's shuttle driver will take you right to your car.

Take Along Your Contacts

When you travel for business, bring all the phone numbers, fax numbers, e-mail addresses, and other information for all your colleagues and clients. If one of them leaves a message on your office voice mail, you'll be able to return the call efficiently even if your caller failed to leave a number.

Make sure your briefcase contains everything you'll need on the road: extra business cards, pens, pencils, a small stapler, a calculator, sticky notes, a notepad, stationery and envelopes for jotting quick thank-yous, blank air bills or preaddressed labels so you can send packages home, large mailing envelopes, postage stamps, a few file folders, and an envelope for travel receipts. If you travel with a laptop computer, consider the accessories you might need, such as an AC adapter and cables, a modem, a phone cord, a spare battery, blank floppy disks, a bootable floppy disk, and a printer cable. Also carry any information related to the programs or online service you'll be using (such as a toll-free number for obtaining local access numbers so you don't have to make a long-distance call to pick up voice mail).

Before you leave, make copies of your itinerary for coworkers, your spouse, or anyone else who may need to reach you.

BUSINESS TRAVEL TOOLS

P ACKING FOR A BUSINESS TRIP can be difficult—not only do you
need to bring the right clothes, you need documents, gadgets,
and office supplies as well. A few simple tools will help you stay
organized while you're in transit.

▲ **A compact** *organizer keeps credit cards, notepad,
and handheld computer consolidated and accessible.*

▶ **A rolling** *carry-on bag (with a front pouch for
your computer) is easy to pull through an airport
and may be small enough to fit under your seat.*

◀ **A garment bag** *keeps your best suit wrinkle-
free and ready for that all-important meeting.*

▼ **A traveler's** *alarm clock will rouse you from
slumber in any time zone.*

Even if you're accessible by pager, take a list of phone numbers. It'll speed things up when it comes time to return calls.

Of course, don't forget the absolute essentials: your tickets, your passport or other documents for foreign travel, your calendar, maps, traveler's checks, credit cards, and any business or personal phone numbers you may need. Remember to carry plenty of small bills for tipping.

ON THE ROAD

Don't fret about time lost while traveling: You can use the travel hours productively. When you're flying, read, catch up on sleep, listen to a training tape, work on a proposal (either on a laptop computer or with pen and paper), fill out your expense report, or make notes about points you want to bring up at your meeting. If you are traveling long distances in your car, take along audiotapes for entertainment or training and a voice-activated mini–tape recorder to dictate notes as you roll along.

It's a good idea to schedule your return trip for late afternoon or early evening so you're winding down at the end of a normal working day. Or return very early in the morning so you can start the day as you would any other. One way to avoid jet lag when you're crossing time zones is to set your watch to the time at your destination. This gets you mentally ready for the new location. Try to sleep en route if your flight lands in the morning; avoid sleeping if it arrives in the evening. And remember to spend time outdoors every day, even if it amounts to nothing more than a short walk outside the hotel.

Eating on the road can pose problems. Short flights have no food service—and often not enough time between flights to purchase a meal. Clients who want to be wined and dined may expect big dinners every night. The solution is to carry healthful, nonperishable snacks such as nuts and dried fruit with you. They can stand in for a meal if you're pressed for time or if you want a light lunch in anticipation of a filling dinner. Too tired to dine out? Use room service or order takeout and kick back in your room with the TV on. If you have a friend or relative in the city you are traveling to, make arrangements ahead of time to treat them to an evening out at one of their favorite restaurants.

There's no need to give up your exercise routine when you travel. If you like to walk or jog, ask the hotel for recommendations about where to go. If you work out with equipment, check with the hotel

Sort as You Go

When you travel, keep in mind that you have only three choices about any document you receive: file it, act on it, or toss it (remember: FAT). Carry a to-file folder for items you'll need to file later (mark filing categories on sticky notes). Also carry an action file for things to do when you return. Toss everything else into the nearest wastebasket.

TIME OUT ON THE ROAD

WHETHER YOU'RE TRAVELING 300 miles from home or 3,000, whether your destination is ordinary or exotic, you can turn a business excursion into a vacation and enjoy the trip. Here are three strategies for having fun on the job.

Simple   Plan your trip for a Monday or Friday and spend the weekend in the area seeing the sights with local friends, relatives, or by yourself. If you stay over the weekend, you can often get a cheaper air fare.

Simpler   Visit museums and other local attractions before you leave town, or catch a show one evening while you're there. Consider getting extra tickets for clients or business associates.

Simplest   Enjoy the luxuries that your hotel offers. Treat yourself to a massage, room service, a game of tennis or golf, or just a quiet night watching in-room movies or soaking in the tub.

before you register to see if it has adequate facilities. An alternative is portable exercise equipment, such as the Fit 10 (see the Resources list on page 143), which is small enough to carry in your suitcase and use inside your hotel room.

If you'll be in the same hotel room for more than one night, set it up so that it's as functional as possible. For instance, you may want to move the desk so you have enough light to write. Put all the advertising for hotel restaurants, local attractions, and hotel movies in a drawer to make the room feel less commercial, and consider carrying a framed photo of your family to put on the bedside table as a reminder of why you're working so hard.

Managing expense reimbursement can be a big headache for business travelers. All those little receipts are easy to lose and sometimes illegible. And it takes time to separate personal expenses from business

expenses or to divide expenses among clients if you have more than one. Have a compartment in your wallet or briefcase where you collect receipts as you get them. Or bring along an envelope if you need more space. More and more companies are using software programs for submitting expenses, so if you carry a laptop, you can enter information as you go. If you use paper forms for submitting expenses, take them with you so you can make entries while you're waiting for a meeting to start or for a flight connection.

When you return home, unpack as soon as possible so you can get back into your normal routine. Spend a few minutes making notes about how to improve your next journey. Was the flight at a good time? Was the rented car large enough? Most important, spend some extra time with your family to recharge yourself and to let them know you missed them.

BIG-TIME STRESS: CHANGING JOBS

———— ✳ ————

WOULDN'T LIFE BE SIMPLE IF YOU HAD THE PERFECT BOSS AND THE PERFECT JOB—CLOSE TO HOME, WELL PAID, CHALLENGING BUT NOT TOO STRESSFUL? SO WHY HAVEN'T YOU BEEN LOOKING FOR SOMETHING BETTER?

If you are feeling bored, unappreciated, or unfulfilled in your present job, don't just stay put. Decreased morale and frustrations at work can spill over into your personal life, creating problems at home. A job that challenges and fulfills you will make you happier all around.

If you're content where you are but talk of a merger or downsizing has your workplace awash with rumors and record-high stress levels, you would be wise to

With a little effort *on your part, you can find the job that offers just the right combination of challenge and reward—with a boss and colleagues who appreciate you.*

investigate other options. Even if you happen to survive the budget ax this time, you may not be so fortunate next time. And the office stress and new workplace dynamics that result from the downsizing may eventually become intolerable.

But how are you going to find your dream job when you're too busy to undertake an extensive search? To get started, browse the Web (when you're away from the office). Extensive databases let you search nationwide based on job titles or other keywords. Many business Web sites post job openings in addition to providing helpful background on the firm. On job sites you simply enter your skills, interests,

SIMPLY PUT...

EMPLOYMENT PROFESSIONALS

employment agency • A business that lists jobs, usually rank-and-file positions in a certain category. Most agencies charge employers a commission; others charge new employees a percentage of their first month's salary.

recruiter • Also known as a head-hunter. These are agents an employer hires to fill executive or managerial positions. The new employee must often stay for a minimum length of time before the recruiter can collect his or her commission.

and requirements in a database employers can search. Some sites allow you to block specific company access so your own employer won't see your information. The best sites provide free listings for job seekers and charge companies a fee for access.

Develop an action plan to get where you want to go. Even if you're not actively looking for a job, update your résumé and consider upgrading your skills. You never know when you might need them. You could take evening classes at your local community college or enroll in a correspondence course from a respected institution. When you're looking for a job, it's essential to network—to get the word out discreetly that you're looking, and to develop helpful contacts. If you remain constantly on the alert for situations in which

you can help other people, it is highly likely that one of those people will return the favor when you need it.

DOWNSIZING

With all the mergers and layoffs going on, it's possible that at some point in your career your job will be eliminated. Ideally, you have a plan in place that provides a financial cushion for just this kind of emergency—such as six months' wages in the bank. If you don't have a safety valve, start planning it now. If you hear that layoffs are coming and you're fairly confident you're targeted, you might approach your supervisor or human resources department and see if you can negotiate a severance package before you're handed a pink slip.

In the event that you lose your job, expect some emotional fallout. Your job may have provided you with your identity or your social network. Research shows that people go through five normal and necessary stages when dealing with a major trauma such as being laid off:

Stage 1. Shock or denial. "How could this happen to me? I'm sure they'll change their mind about closing the plant."

Stage 2. Emotion, usually anger. "How dare they do this to me?"

Stage 3. Bargaining with someone who seems to be in a position of influence. "I'll steer contacts your way if you'll convince the company to take me back."

Stage 4. Grief and depression. "Things never seem to work out for me."

Stage 5. Acceptance and forward momentum. "This is really disappointing, but I'm sure I can find a better job."

Identify the stage you are in and nurture yourself physically, emotionally, and spiritually through the transition from one state to another. One of life's ironies is that often the best way to maintain your edge is to relax. Taking time for fun and renewing social contacts can provide the energy you need to get through this crisis.

Although we all resist change, many people ultimately find that losing a job is the best thing that ever happened to them. They might switch to an entirely new career, making more money in a position that provides more pleasure. They might go back to school or become entrepreneurs, pursuing a dream they wouldn't have dared to aim for without a push.

FINDING A JOB

If you've decided to find a new job, either in the same field or a new one, you'll have to face the task we all dread—the job hunt. Finding work is time-consuming, nerve-racking, and humbling. It helps to remember that searching for a job is difficult for everyone and that it takes time to find a new position. You can expect to spend between three and six months on a search for a new job—longer if you're seeking a higher-level position. If you don't have the resources to pay the bills during that time, consider freelance, temporary, or part-time work. It might not be in the field you're pursuing, but it'll get you out of the house and earning money.

In your search, think of how an employer likes to hire for a position. Most prefer to hire someone they know—or a friend or a colleague knows. Employers are wary of an unknown applicant—even if a résumé is impressive, there may be hidden problems, such as an uncontrolled temper or a tendency to call in sick. So network as much as you can. Approach everyone you've ever met in your field of business and let them know what you're looking for. If you can call a potential employer and say that someone he or she trusts suggested you get in touch, you're in a much better position than someone who simply sent in a résumé.

Another job-hunt tactic can be helpful when you've targeted some companies but there are no positions currently available.

Put on your thinking cap and dream up ways you can sell your skills to potential employers.

Speeding Up a Job Hunt

WHEN YOU'RE LOOKING FOR a job, it may be tempting to take the easy route and phone a recruiter or an agency. But remember: They're working for the employer and don't have your best interest at heart. Widening your search—though more complex and difficult—will have you back at work sooner doing a job you love.

Take a temporary job. You're looking for a permanent position, so you might think a temporary job will prevent you from accepting that eventual offer. But most employers prefer to hire their temporary or part-time employees for permanent, full-time positions, so when a slot opens, you'll be first in line. In the meantime, you'll also be gaining more experience and earning needed cash.

Network. Tell everyone you know—whether they're in your field of business or not—that you're looking for a job. Mention it to your hairdresser, your doctor, your neighbor, your friends. The more people you have looking on your behalf, the better your chances of finding the job you want quickly.

Forget the want ads. Only a minority of all jobs are ever advertised in the newspaper. Most employers fill their positions by promoting from within, soliciting recommendations from colleagues, using a recruiter, or hiring someone they already know. And don't limit your search to only those companies that you've heard are seeking to fill a spot: Employers you approach may be planning to create a position for someone with exactly your skills.

Be persistent. If a company you're interested in working for has no spots available the first time you approach it, try again a few months later. Someone may have left, or a job may have been created. Even if you've applied for an opening and been rejected, don't give up on the company. The management may have changed its mind in the interim about the kind of candidate that it is seeking.

Target smaller companies. Job seekers often make the mistake of focusing only on the Fortune 500. But the vast majority of jobs being created are with smaller companies, especially growing ones. In fact, larger companies are responsible for most of the downsizing. With a smaller company, you're also more likely to reach the people doing the hiring rather than be sent to the personnel department—often a dead end.

Make cold calls. Target companies in your field or the field in which you're searching, find the name of someone in a position to hire you, take a deep breath, and dial the phone. Introduce yourself and your experience and explain why you're interested in that company. The employer will be impressed with your resourcefulness, and this may give you a leg up on other applicants if a job is available.

Use the Internet. Go online to find companies in your field, get information about firms you're interested in, or check a company's Web site for job listings. Many employment agencies also list job openings online, but unless you're in a high-demand field like technology, these listings are about as productive as the want ads. Once you've found a prospect, you can use e-mail to send in your résumé or to reach contacts who are inaccessible by phone.

Join a support group. It's hard to keep your spirits up when you're rejected time and again. A job-searching support group will lift your spirits by showing you you're not alone. Your fellow job seekers also might have some tips for finding work or even valuable job leads.

Try to set up an informational interview with someone who would be in a position to hire you. You'll get acquainted, and the person will be more likely to have you in mind when a position does open up. Bring a list of relevant questions and be sure to keep your interview brief.

SURVIVING INTERVIEWS

The job you've always wanted is finally available, but now you face an even bigger hurdle—the interview. It's hardly news that interviews cause stress. You're seeking the approval of another person, in all likelihood someone you don't know—but as with a public presentation, preparation is the key. Research the company thoroughly (or the department, if the new job is within your own company). Talk with other people who work there, if possible, to get an idea of what the employer is seeking.

Remember that the interview is your chance to find out if the job is for you. Ask questions of the employer and evaluate the environment. Note the following to get a sense of how comfortable you'd be there:

◆ HOW DO PEOPLE DRESS?

◆ ARE OFFICE DOORS MOSTLY
   OPEN OR CLOSED?

◆ WHAT KIND OF TECHNOLOGY
   DO PEOPLE USE?

◆ ARE EMPLOYEES TALKING
   TO ONE ANOTHER?

In preparing for an interview, be able to explain clearly why you want to work at the company and why you're interested in the particular position. Know what your strengths are and the impression you want to give about yourself. Formulate answers

In an interview, *try to listen at least as much as you talk. The employer will be pleased that you are interested in the company.*

to questions you may be asked and practice your responses—out loud. Being able to answer a question in your head doesn't ensure it will come out of your mouth as you intended. But don't overrehearse to the point of sounding insincere.

Always arrive a little early. Keep in mind that anyone with whom you come into contact—including the receptionist or the fellow at the water fountain—may have input into the hiring decision, so behave professionally at all times. Finally, always send a prompt thank-you note.

Whenever you start to feel desperate in your search, remember that you're shopping for a better job, not just looking for someone to hire you. It's worth your while to wait for a good offer. You don't want to end up in the same situation that caused you to start your search in the first place.

WHEN YOU'RE
ON your Own

1 Maintain your **focus** with a daily work schedule, child-care arrangements, and safeguards against distractions. **2** Try to be **sensitive** to the spatial and emotional needs of others in your home. **3** Support your efforts with a team of **experts** to assist you— an accountant, a lawyer, a computer whiz, and others. **4** If you telecommute, ask your employer for clear **guidelines** regarding your role and responsibilities. **5** Create your ideal home office by finding the perfect **location,** furniture, and lighting for your needs. **6** When setting up your home office, make use of **ergonomic** designs to protect yourself from fatigue and injury. **7** Do your homework to ensure you choose the right phone, fax, copier, and computer **equipment.** **8** Identify nearby business **resources** (copy shops, office-supply stores, courier services) so you'll know where they are when you need them. **9** Combat the isolation of **working solo** by staying in touch with business associates and joining professional organizations. ●

WORKING AT HOME

**SIMPLIFYING LIFE WHEN
YOUR HOME IS YOUR OFFICE**

✳ —— ✳ —— ✳

Working at a job in the convenience of your home—whether you're running a business or employed by someone else—can definitely increase the potential for job satisfaction.

Think of it! No more sitting in smoggy traffic lanes or fighting for a seat on the bus. If you choose, you can start your day at 5 A.M., take a break to get the kids off to school, then finish up in time for the bus that delivers them back home. Or head to the gym in the morning, start your work-day after lunch, and go until midnight.

Working at home provides terrific benefits—but it also poses great challenges. Choosing the right equipment, coping with a staff of none, meeting your own deadlines and goals, and overcoming feelings of isolation require ingenuity and resourcefulness. Some simple strategies can make your home office a stress-free place to work and turn your job into a joy.

DOING IT YOUR WAY

--- ✳ ---

ACCORDING TO RECENT STUDIES, MORE THAN 15 MILLION PEOPLE IN THE UNITED STATES WORK AT HOME AT LEAST ONE DAY A WEEK. THEY EITHER RUN THEIR OWN BUSINESSES OR TELECOMMUTE TO THEIR BUSINESSES AND JOBS.

Being able to spend the day in your own space, in charge of your own time, may well simplify your workday enormously.

Your home can be absolutely user friendly, from the comfortable dress code to the convenient leftovers stashed in your refrigerator. You can plow through your in box without the usual dozens of distractions. Running errands is a breeze compared with the elaborate juggling you used to do to get those chores done. And the time you save on commuting—you just step from the bedroom to your home office—is the icing on the cake. But not

everyone who works at home finds it easy to manage this newfound freedom: Some people have trouble taking care of business when there's a pile of laundry to do and a lawn to mow. You'll need to be resourceful to make it all work for you.

STAYING FOCUSED

The good news about working at home is that you'll be there when the repair people arrive to fix the furnace or when your cat needs to go to the vet. But that's also the bad news. Focusing on your job when distractions are occurring all around you is

Dressing as you please is one of the simple pleasures of working at home.

one of the major challenges of working at home. These diversions can quickly take over your day unless you establish routines and set limits to protect your priorities and get the job done.

Stay on track by setting a daily work schedule with a regular starting and quitting time. Of course, you can bend it for special circumstances as needed, but the basic structure will help keep you focused. Think about your natural inclinations as

One of the major challenges of working at home is convincing friends and relatives that you aren't available on a moment's notice.

you set about making your schedule. Are you an early bird or a night owl? Do you thrive on a brief afternoon nap? If the nature of your work and the schedules of others in the house permit it, capitalize on your most productive hours. If you work with people in different time zones, keep that in mind when planning.

Some people find that dressing the part helps them get into work mode. You don't need to wear a suit and tie—business casual will do the trick. On the other hand, you may not need to give a single thought to your wardrobe. Lots of people who work at home are thrilled that they can wear pajamas while they're talking to important customers or the boss.

One of the major challenges of working at home is convincing friends and relatives that you are actually busy and not available for babysitting or driving them

Drawing the Line

To enforce regular starting and quitting times in your workday, schedule an activity each morning and evening as a stand-in for your "commute." You can take a walk every morning, for example, and in the evening pick up mail at your post office box. These activities can help you draw a clear dividing line between your workday and your home life.

to the mechanic on a moment's notice. The simplest solution is to have a separate business phone (give this number to business contacts only) and let your answering machine or voice mail pick up your personal line. You'll still be able to monitor personal calls in case there's an emergency that requires your immediate attention.

FAMILY MATTERS

Your children may well be a major reason you're working at home, but don't delude yourself into thinking that job and family will blend seamlessly. In many situations, the home office and children mix like oil and water. You'll be annoyed by all their interruptions, and your kids will be frustrated they don't have your full attention. If your home business is only a part-time endeavor, you may be able to accomplish everything while the kids are napping, at school, or playing with friends. But seasoned home office pros, especially those

A separate space *for your home office, however small, helps you keep work and home life from interfering with each other.*

using the same office space may be workable—or even desirable. But if the parties have totally unrelated jobs, separate offices (perhaps with some shared equipment) are probably better. In either case, each person needs a separate desk area.

Tolerance and sensitivity are also crucial if one of you works in a home office and the other one works outside. Having spent the day alone, the at-home worker will probably be eager for a little social interaction. The spouse who works outside the home and has just completed a lengthy commute typically wants some peace and quiet at the end of the day.

who work full-time, often find that the best solution is to keep the family and the office separate. This may mean taking the kids to day care or hiring a babysitter (or utilizing your spouse) to keep them safe and happy in another part of the house or at the neighborhood park.

Additional challenges arise if both you and your spouse work at home. It seems like such a simple idea—two compatible people sharing the same space. But even couples in highly successful relationships discover a few unwelcome surprises. Your spouse may be on the phone constantly, for example, while you spend your time reading reports. Or you may find that your relationship suffers from too much togetherness. Working out these problems successfully requires constant communication.

If both parties are in the same business, and thus share the same objectives,

THE ENTREPRENEUR

Running a business from your home will undoubtedly require a few skills that you don't have. Assembling a team of experts to rely on will keep you up-to-date so you can focus on your own field of expertise.

Two additions to your company team—a lawyer and an accountant—may well be worthwhile. Although several available software packages can help you draw up contracts and other legal documents, your lawyer can provide the final check to make sure that you've covered all bases. And should you decide to incorporate your business, he or she can easily handle the necessary paperwork.

Your accountant can offer accurate advice regarding complicated tax issues you must handle appropriately in order to avoid liability. Additionally, your accountant will provide regular reports that summarize the health of your business. If you need insurance to protect the business, an insurance broker can advise you, as well as recommend health and disability insurance for you and any employees.

Another important team member, a computer professional, can advise you on appropriate hardware and software for your work, provide training, and come to the rescue when your system goes down.

If you hire employees who work at your home, check out the zoning laws in your neighborhood, as well as your home-owner and business insurance policies. Some areas have no problem with your hiring one person, but don't allow other employees or customers to come to the office. Zoning laws may also govern delivery trucks, manufacturing, and signage.

TELECOMMUTING

A growing number of people are going home to work for their companies, either a few days a week or full-time. Telecommuting saves businesses money on overhead and office space and lets them hire

Cover Yourself

Most homeowner insurance policies exclude business activities, so if a client or a vendor trips over your doormat and breaks a leg, you won't be covered. Talk with an insurance agent about adding a rider to your existing homeowner's policy or purchasing a special policy in order to get the coverage you need for your home-based business.

qualified workers who are not willing to relocate. For workers, telecommuting typically saves time and money by eliminating the commute and cutting down on an

Working at home *is a satisfying alternative for many people. You arrange your own hours and fit in errands or exercise as you choose.*

expensive business wardrobe. The flexi-bility that telecommuting offers can also make it easier to arrange child care—or to eliminate the need for it altogether.

So why isn't everyone doing it? While recent surveys claim that the ranks of tele-commuters swell by 20 percent a year, they also reveal that only four-fifths of those who try the experiment succeed. Why do the others fail? In some cases, the employee misses the social climate or the opportuni-ties for advancement at the office. But in many other instances, the reason for failure

has nothing to do with the person who's working at home: The job just may not be well suited for telecommuting, or the manager might not know how to manage employees effectively off-site.

Reach a clear understanding with your supervisor about how the success of your telecommuting arrangement will be measured.

Your chances for successful telecommuting will improve if you do the following:

Know your status. Clarify whether you are an employee or a contractor in order to assess tax liabilities and be certain what, if any, benefits you'll receive.

Learn the policies. Obtain a written document describing company policies and procedures for working at home.

Use a yardstick. Reach a clear under-standing with your supervisor about how the company will measure the success of your telecommuting arrangement.

Make yourself available. Be sure you're on hand to receive calls from your boss.

Put in an appearance. Attend regular meetings at company headquarters with your supervisor and colleagues.

Get the right tools. Purchase the equip-ment and supplies that you need to do the job efficiently—or have your employer supply these materials for you.

Obtain support. If your company has an information systems department, find out if it will assist you in your home office. Be sure you know whom to call when the need arises—because it will!

SIMPLY PUT...

EMPLOYEE VERSUS CONTRACTOR

employee • A person who works for a wage or fixed payment. The em-ployer withholds taxes and Social Se-curity from pay, may offer benefits such as paid vacation and sick leave, and determines the employee's work con-ditions (when, how, and where). The employer's workers' compensation covers injuries suffered on the job.

independent contractor A worker who receives full payment from clients and pays his or her own taxes, as well as both the employer and employee portion of Social Secu-rity. Time off is unpaid. A contractor sets his or her own hours, provides the tools and work space, and is not covered by the workers' compensa-tion insurance of clients.

HOME OFFICE BASICS

*

ONCE YOU'VE LAID THE GROUNDWORK FOR YOUR HOME-BASED BUSINESS OR TELECOMMUTING PLAN, TAKE TIME TO CHOOSE A SPOT IN YOUR HOME WHERE YOU'LL ENJOY WORKING, DAY IN AND DAY OUT.

The basement that at first seems like the ideal solution because of its privacy could become depressing if it's too dark and damp. With the advent of family rooms, more people are turning underused spaces such as living rooms and formal dining rooms into practical, pleasant offices. Be certain the space works for you, as well as for the other members of your household. Confining your office to a well-defined area separate from the family's living space is essential. It's important that you—and the rest of the family—be able to tell when you leave the office.

As you make your selection, also keep in mind the requirements of your business. Do clients need to come see you in your office, or would meeting them at a nearby coffee shop work just as well—while also providing an excuse for you to get out? Do you need space for inventory near your work area, or can you do the bulk of the work in your favorite place and use a less desirable part of the house for storage?

Don't overlook the importance of lighting. If you'll be spending much of your day on a computer, a sunny room that seems inviting may be a bad choice

A home office needn't be a grand space—just a location that's comfortable.

Document holder

If you do a lot of complex data entry, such as creating tables or lists, you'll benefit from a document holder. It keeps your papers upright and close to eye level so you can see them easily without craning your neck. Its sliding guide shows you your place; a clip at the top keeps papers from slipping out.

Angled keyboard

Many people find that the classic rectangular keyboard forces their hands and wrists into an uncomfortable position. This ergonomic model splits the keys used by the left and right hands to form a more natural angle for typing. It also has a built-in platform to help provide support for your wrists.

Ergonomic mouse pad

A mouse pad with a wrist support helps keep your hand and forearm on the same plane, reducing stress to your tendons and wrist.

Ergonomic mouse

A mouse that fits the contours of your hand is more comfortable and easier to use than one with a flatter profile. Mouse devices come in many ergonomic forms, including one with a trackball that lets you guide the on-screen cursor with your fingertips.

because of glare on the screen. If you want to work there, you may need to install blinds or drapes. Similarly, a room that is too dark may feel confining or cut down on work efficiency. Make sure that you have enough lighting in each task area.

FURNITURE

Having the right furniture makes your job much easier. Start with a desk or tabletop that provides plenty of space for your daily activities. If you'll be dealing with paper, make sure your desk has at least one file drawer. If it doesn't, set up a portable file box close by your desk.

The home office boom has resulted in a wide variety of furniture choices, including custom-designed and built-in home office cabinetry. Some combination units are even designed so you can fold them out of sight at the end of the day—or at least when company comes.

To save money, check the Yellow Pages for companies that liquidate used office furniture. They often have merchandise of excellent quality at a reasonable price. Read the newspaper classified ads for business liquidations or auctions. Also comb flea markets, thrift shops, garage sales, and even businesses undergoing renovations for useful possibilities. If you can find furniture that needs only a little sandpaper and paint, you've got a great bargain.

Your chair will be the foundation for a comfortable workday, so it makes sense to splurge and get the best one you can afford. Its backrest should arch forward to support the natural S curve of your spine, relieving pressure on your lower back. The seat height should let your feet rest flat on the floor, to take pressure off the back of your thighs. If it doesn't, use a footrest.

Any other people who work in your office, even on a part-time basis, will need a comfortable spot to do their job. If customers will be dropping by, you'll want to provide a place for them to sit, maybe even a small waiting area. And consider a refreshment center for serving drinks and snacks—perhaps a coffeemaker and a small microwave and refrigerator.

Whatever you choose, be certain to arrange your office efficiently. An easy way to experiment with floor plans is to do them first on paper or on a computer. Use graph paper or a home-decorating program to make a scale drawing of your space and all the furniture and equipment. You can then easily rearrange the pieces, considering entrances, traffic patterns, natural lighting, and so forth.

Look for office furnishings that will provide maximum comfort.

TOOLS FOR YOUR WORK

Communicating easily with colleagues and customers is key to streamlining your work, so take some time to identify your telephone needs. Using your personal phone for business purposes is rarely a smart idea. In fact, many home workers find that *two* additional business lines are essential: one for voice and another for fax and online access. If you want to save costs and use your personal phone, you can pay for a distinctive ringing service from your telephone company. This enables you to program your phone to recognize incoming callers you specify, and to ring in a distinctive way. Thus, you'll know when important business associates are calling.

A cordless phone may be a wise choice if you want to be able to move around your office or home while you're talking, or sit on your patio on a nice day—but purchase

Companies that liquidate office furniture often have excellent prices. Thrift shops and garage sales can also yield great bargains.

well-made equipment so you don't sacrifice sound quality. If you spend a large portion of your day on the phone—or if you need to take notes while you talk—a headset is preferable to a traditional handset. These are also available in cordless models.

When it comes to computers, you may be tempted to buy the latest and

All in One

Multifunction office equipment can save money while occupying less space on your desk. These machines typically combine an ink-jet printer, a fax machine, a copier, and even a scanner in a package no larger than most printers. The downside is that if you have to send such a device to the repair shop, you're out of business while you wait.

greatest, but make certain the benefits clearly outweigh the costs. Doing your homework is essential in order to get the best return on your investment. Decide first how you will be using the computer, then determine the appropriate software for the job. If you need advice, talk with

Beware of buying more software than you really need. Underused applications waste money as well as space on your hard drive.

a computer consultant, your clients, or service bureaus to determine what hardware and software are compatible with your requirements. You may decide to hire someone to customize your software to meet special business needs by adding macros or industry-specific templates. If you have children, think about whether they will be using your computer for their

homework or entertainment. However, be aware that your equipment may not be fully tax deductible if they do.

When buying software, consider purchasing an office suite or individual programs that work easily with your existing applications. This ease of integration is extremely useful for creating complex reports and presentations (see page 82 for more guidance). And consistent menus flatten the learning curve—learn one set of menus, and you can apply them in other suite applications as well. But beware of buying more software than you really need. Underused applications waste your money as well as space on your hard drive.

Don't forget that all this equipment uses electricity. Consider whether you have enough voltage coming into your home to supply your computer, printer, copier, and other equipment. Also purchase a surge suppressor or a UPS (see page 87) to guard against sudden power fluctuations.

STAYING SLIM

Of course, you may not need some equipment, especially if it's expensive and you won't use it often. For instance, you can fax with your computer modem instead of buying a fax machine. Or you can do occasional photocopying at a copy shop rather than buy a copier of your own. Keep a list of vendors for additional services, such as printing and delivery. Use your rotary card file or contact management program to track the businesses that provide the kinds of services you need— and the hours they are open, in case you're working on a late-night project.

HOME OFFICE FURNISHINGS

O NE ADVANTAGE OF WORKING AT HOME is that your office doesn't have to look like one—unless you want it to. You can purchase business furnishings if those work for you, or you can use household items to hold your filing and hide your papers.

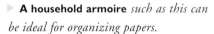
▲ **A wire-frame drawer system** *keeps your work visible while storing it neatly.*

▶ **A household armoire** *such as this can be ideal for organizing papers.*

▲ **In an office** *in your bedroom, baskets store papers more attractively than a file cabinet.*

◀ **If a corner** *of your living room serves as an office, a screen will hide your work space when you're off duty or while you're entertaining.*

You Are Not Alone

※

At first it may seem terrific to be on your own, working where and how you please. Wow! No tiresome commute. No more distracting interruptions, unnecessary memos, or nonstop phone calls.

Several weeks later, though, you may notice you're on the phone with the old office gang on a regular basis. And what do you want to hear about? What everyone is up to, not only in the office, but on their weekends as well. What's going on? You're experiencing the symptoms of withdrawal from the social scene. Human resources experts find that people often underestimate their need for social and professional contact. In fact, isolation is a major reason that telecommuting fails.

If you're working solo and find yourself chatting away to the dog, it may be time to get out and about. Pack your schedule with lunch dates, breakfast get-togethers, and afternoon workouts with friends. Don't underestimate the importance of getting outdoors now and then, even if it's to walk the dog. The change of scenery, the gentle stretching of your limbs, and perhaps a friendly chat with a neighbor or shopkeeper can rev you up for the challenges ahead.

If you're still feeling lonely and you have sufficient space in your house, you might consider renting a spare room to another solitary home worker.

BUILDING A NETWORK

Many people find that working at home is not just lonely—they miss the professional contacts: information about competitors, news of developments in their fields, even advice from a mentor or supervisor.

If you're starting your own business, you'll find that making contacts is essential, not only to obtain customers but also to learn from people with experience in your line of business. Consider establishing a board of advisers. Ask them to meet with you perhaps once a month to give you feedback in exchange for lunch—either as a group or separately—at a time that's convenient for them. Successful businesspeople are often very willing to give their assistance to those just starting out.

A Bird in the Hand

It's five times more costly to close a sale with a new client than it is to sell additional services to an existing one. Keep in touch with the clients who have used your services in the past by phoning them occasionally, sending them e-mail, or mailing them postcards, relevant clippings (with a quick note), or even a newsletter of your own.

If the home audience is bored with your pitch, it's time to get out and about.

In searching for customers, don't overlook the less obvious methods. You may be able to form alliances and exchange leads with businesses that have common ground with yours but don't compete for the same set of customers. For instance, if you operate a housecleaning service, a real estate agent in your area might be happy to recommend you to new homeowners, display your business cards in his or her office, or even hire you to spruce up a house that's going on the market. In return, you can hand out the agent's card when a client wants to buy or sell a house.

Make a conscious effort to network with just about everyone you encounter throughout the day—your hairdresser, your child's preschool teacher, your auto mechanic. Be sure they know what kind of work you do. Concentrate on how you can help them build their business as well. If you're able to do them a favor, they're much more likely keep you in mind when they meet someone who could use the service or product your business offers.

JOINING UP

Informal opportunities for networking are all around you, but you'll want to pursue more formal avenues as well.

A great place to start is by joining a professional association. For a nominal annual fee you usually get regular updates on issues affecting your industry and the chance to join others at meetings or conventions. Your local chamber of commerce may have regular events designed to help businesspeople get to know each other.

At any get-together, remember that you're building relationships. Networking gurus like Harvey Mackay, author of several books on the subject (see page 142), emphasize how important it is to keep track of people's personal details. Ask that fellow you met at lunch how his daughter likes college, or that seminar speaker how her vacation in Cancún went. Attention to detail can make the difference between a casual encounter soon forgotten and the start of a long-term business relationship.

How do you remember all that information? If you get a business card from a new acquaintance, quickly jot down pertinent data on the back of the card. The tool of the day for making it simple—and powerful—is a contact manager program (see page 93), perhaps on a PDA.

Another trick for working the crowd is to use the buddy system. Seek out someone you know and have him or her introduce you to others. Do the same in return: Introduce your buddy to someone, then exit so they can get acquainted.

Perhaps the most important thing to remember is that many, if not most, of the people at networking events are even more apprehensive than you are. You can make a great impression just by helping other people feel comfortable, so conquer your shyness. Be your own welcoming committee: If you attend a monthly mixer, chat with the people you already know, then introduce yourself to one or two new acquaintances. Before too long, you'll know everyone in the room. (For more tips on starting a business, see page 141.)

In your efforts to build your business, don't get so caught up in work that you neglect your family or fail to take care of your health. Even though you'll almost certainly have to put in long hours promoting and conducting your business, set aside time to relax, exercise, and have fun. If you take the stress out of your work life today, you'll be guaranteeing yourself a much more enjoyable tomorrow.

(For more tips on starting a business, see page 141.)

SIMPLE SOLUTIONS

BUSINESS CARD DESIGN

Your BUSINESS CARDS don't need to be elaborate to make a good impression. In fact, a simple, straightforward design usually looks more professional than a design filled with mismatched type and a hodgepodge of graphics. A few easy alternatives:

Simple   Buy business-card stock for laser printers and print your own cards, using a page layout program or the label-printing feature on your word processor. That way you can print only as many cards as you need.

Simpler   Work with a graphic artist who can design the cards for you and supervise the printing. Quick-print shops often have a designer on staff, or they can refer you to one they work with regularly.

Simplest   Order cards in a predesigned format from an office-supply store or mail-order catalog. Some sources offer a selection of layouts, typefaces, ink colors, and logos appropriate to various businesses.

CHECKLISTS AND RESOURCES

INFORMATION THAT WORKS FOR YOU

* —— ✳ —— *

Reducing your level of stress while you're on the job depends as much on strong organizational skills as it does on good people skills. In the pages that follow, you will find 11 handy lists and forms to hone both kinds of skills and help keep you on top of the more difficult and stress-inducing aspects of your workday—whether you run a business from your home or manage a group of people in an office.

You'll discover an assortment of pointers, checklists, and blank worksheets that you can photocopy to use again and again. Employ them to get a handle on everything from prioritizing your daily agenda to planning entire projects, from organizing your file drawers to packing for business trips and making important presentations.

The resources listed at the end of this chapter will steer you toward additional information and useful products that can make your work life more productive and stress-free.

EFFECTIVE TIME MANAGEMENT

KEEPING GOALS IN SIGHT

---*---

I T'S EASY TO GET SIDETRACKED BY DAY-TO-DAY DEMANDS, SO IT'S CRUCIAL TO PRIORITIZE YOUR TASKS. FOLLOW THESE POINTERS TO STREAMLINE YOUR WORKDAY AND YOU'LL STAY HEADED TOWARD YOUR GOALS.

◆ Put your goals in writing to remind yourself of your highest priorities.

◆ Buy and use organizational tools such as an appointment book or time-management software.

◆ Keep a master to-do list and refer to it every day.

◆ Schedule your to-dos, along with personal errands, in your daily planner.

◆ Invest the time necessary to organize your work area.

◆ Determine the next action for paperwork as soon as it lands on your desk.

◆ Use strategies to prevent procrastination, such as breaking down tasks into small, manageable pieces.

◆ Restrict the amount of time you spend on less important tasks by setting a timer or an alarm clock.

◆ Take breaks to clear your mind and give you more energy to finish your work.

◆ Avoid interruptions by sending phone calls to voice mail or hanging a "Busy" sign on the back of your chair.

◆ Delegate responsibilities, where appropriate, to others who can free you for higher-priority assignments.

◆ Learn to say no when you can't take on extra assignments.

◆ Carefully evaluate your options before you make a decision. But don't linger— it's usually better to act.

◆ Schedule lunches with friends outside the office to gain new perspectives on work situations.

◆ Complete at least one task each day that will take you toward your long-term goals.

◆ Reward yourself and coworkers when you reach interim goals and deadlines.

◆ Spend 10 to 15 minutes at the end of each day planning your priorities for the next day.

MASTER TO-DO LIST

A WORKSHEET FOR PRIORITIZING TASKS

---※---

Too little time, too much to do? Prioritize by listing each task and checking A, B, C, or D for "Must Do," "Should Do," "Could Do," or "Want to Do." Then put the most urgent tasks on your daily to-do list.

TASK	A Must Do	B Should Do	C Could Do	D Want to Do
	☐	☐	☐	☐
	☐	☐	☐	☐
	☐	☐	☐	☐
	☐	☐	☐	☐
	☐	☐	☐	☐
	☐	☐	☐	☐
	☐	☐	☐	☐
	☐	☐	☐	☐
	☐	☐	☐	☐
	☐	☐	☐	☐
	☐	☐	☐	☐
	☐	☐	☐	☐
	☐	☐	☐	☐
	☐	☐	☐	☐
	☐	☐	☐	☐
	☐	☐	☐	☐
	☐	☐	☐	☐
	☐	☐	☐	☐
	☐	☐	☐	☐
	☐	☐	☐	☐
	☐	☐	☐	☐
	☐	☐	☐	☐
	☐	☐	☐	☐
	☐	☐	☐	☐
	☐	☐	☐	☐
	☐	☐	☐	☐

PROJECT WORKSHEET

MANAGING TASKS EFFICIENTLY

———— ✳ ————

KEEPING PROJECTS ON TIME AND ON TRACK REQUIRES ABSOLUTE CLARITY ABOUT WHO DOES WHAT WHEN AND IN WHICH ORDER. USE THIS FORM TO HELP YOU PLAN—MAKE AS MANY COPIES AS YOU NEED TO LIST EVERY TASK.

PROJECT TITLE

Participants:_____

_____

_____

_____

_____

_____

_____

Project start date:_____
Project end date:_____

TASK NUMBER_____
Description:_____

_____

_____

_____

Who does it:_____
Phone:_____
Do after which task?_____

Do before which task?_____

Workdays to complete:_____
Start date:_____
End date:_____

TASK NUMBER_____
Description:_____

_____

_____

Who does it:_____
Phone:_____
Do after which task?_____

Do before which task?_____

Workdays to complete:_____
Start date:_____
End date:_____

TASK NUMBER_____
Description:_____

_____

_____

Who does it:_____
Phone:_____
Do after which task?_____

Do before which task?_____

Workdays to complete:_____
Start date:_____
End date:_____

TASK NUMBER _____
Description:_____
_____
_____

Who does it:_____
Phone:_____
Do after which task?_____
_____

Do before which task?_____
_____

Workdays to complete:_____
Start date:_____
End date:_____

TASK NUMBER _____
Description:_____
_____
_____

Who does it:_____
Phone:_____
Do after which task?_____
_____

Do before which task?_____
_____

Workdays to complete:_____
Start date:_____
End date:_____

TASK NUMBER _____
Description:_____
_____
_____

Who does it:_____
Phone:_____
Do after which task?_____
_____

Do before which task?_____

Workdays to complete:_____
Start date:_____
End date:_____

TASK NUMBER _____
Description:_____
_____

Who does it:_____
Phone:_____
Do after which task?_____
_____

Do before which task?_____

Workdays to complete:_____
Start date:_____
End date:_____

TASK NUMBER _____
Description:_____
_____

Who does it:_____
Phone:_____
Do after which task?_____

Do before which task?_____

Workdays to complete:_____
Start date:_____
End date:_____

*Notes:*_____
_____
_____
_____

Streamlining Meetings

WAYS TO MAKE GATHERINGS PRODUCTIVE

———— ✳ ————

Time invested in preparing for a meeting will pay off in a focused discussion that accomplishes the agenda in record time. If you're running the meeting, follow these pointers to keep it on track.

◆ Invite only the key people involved.

◆ Circulate an agenda several days before the meeting date and give a deadline for attendees' feedback.

◆ Set a time limit for each agenda item and stick to it.

◆ Assign each agenda item to a person who will be responsible for it.

◆ Schedule several meetings back-to-back to clear a block of time when other work can get done.

◆ Schedule an appointment directly after the last meeting to ensure that the meeting will wrap up on time.

◆ Bring pen, paper, and your appointment book to the meeting so you can note any essential information.

◆ If the attendees arrive from different offices, give them five minutes to socialize before starting the meeting.

◆ Assign someone to take minutes.

◆ Always start the meeting right on time, even if some people haven't yet arrived.

◆ Allow each person a set amount of time to speak.

◆ Have someone watch the clock to make sure the agenda is on track.

◆ Try to involve everyone attending: Ask questions of someone who's not contributing.

◆ If the purpose of the meeting is to have a brainstorming session, make a rule that no one can shoot down an idea.

◆ Focus on making decisions rather than simply continuing discussion.

◆ Table for another meeting any topics that aren't on the agenda.

◆ Make sure that the minutes detail the commitments agreed to, and distribute the minutes to all who attended.

◆ After each meeting, ask yourself how you could have run it more smoothly.

ORGANIZING YOUR OFFICE

TIPS FOR KEEPING YOUR OFFICE IN SHAPE

---✴---

MAINTAINING A FIT AND TRIM WORK SPACE IS AN ONGOING PROCESS. IF YOU SET UP ORGANIZED SYSTEMS AND DO REGULAR HOUSEKEEPING, YOUR WORK WILL FLOW MORE EFFICIENTLY FROM YOUR IN BOX TO YOUR OUT BOX.

◆ Visit an office-supply store (or study its catalog) to find organizing tools.

◆ Be ruthless with your incoming mail— toss as much as possible.

◆ Keep files for current projects in a convenient place.

◆ Develop a consistent naming system for computer files so you can easily find and retrieve what you need.

◆ Keep names and numbers of business associates close to the phone and keep speed-dial numbers up-to-date.

◆ Tape business cards into a rotary card file or scan them into a database.

◆ Label notebooks, shelves, and file cabinets so that you can quickly access and refile important resources.

◆ Keep your file cabinet within easy reach and set aside daily time for filing.

◆ File documents in a few large files rather than in many small files.

◆ Date all filed papers so you can quickly determine if they are outdated.

◆ Give your files names that will be easy to recall when you need them later.

◆ Maintain a file index to help you locate files quickly and easily.

◆ Set up retention guidelines so you know how long to keep each file.

◆ Purge files regularly so the information in them is current and easy to find.

◆ Archive papers you need for legal reasons and send them to off-site storage.

Bask in the glow of a well-tended office.

OFFICE ESSENTIALS

A CHECKLIST OF TOOLS AND SUPPLIES

———————— ✴ ————————

KEEP YOUR WORKDAY HUMMING BY HAVING ON HAND THE ESSENTIAL TOOLS AND SUPPLIES. PLACE ITEMS YOU USE FREQUENTLY WITHIN EASY REACH AND STORE OTHERS NEATLY IN A DESK DRAWER OR ON A CONVENIENT SHELF.

TOOLS

- ☐ Binders—three-ring
- ☐ Calculator
- ☐ Calendar—desk or wall
- ☐ Clipboard
- ☐ Copyholder
- ☐ Desk clock
- ☐ Dividers or trays for drawers
- ☐ File boxes or trays—In/Out/To File
- ☐ Hanging file frames
- ☐ Letter opener
- ☐ Paper cutter
- ☐ Pen/pencil cup
- ☐ Pencil sharpener
- ☐ Petty cash box
- ☐ Planner/calendar system
- ☐ Postal scale
- ☐ Recycling box
- ☐ Rotary card file
- ☐ Ruler
- ☐ Scissors
- ☐ Stamp for dating incoming paperwork
- ☐ Stamp for endorsing checks
- ☐ Staple remover
- ☐ Stapler
- ☐ Storage unit for computer disks
- ☐ Tape dispenser
- ☐ Three-hole punch
- ☐ Wastebasket

SUPPLIES

- ☐ Blank floppy disks
- ☐ Business cards
- ☐ Correction fluid
- ☐ Envelopes—#10 business, letterhead
- ☐ Envelopes—#10 business, plain
- ☐ Envelopes—manila
- ☐ Files—hanging
- ☐ Files—manila file folders
- ☐ Glue sticks
- ☐ Labels—address
- ☐ Labels—file folder
- ☐ Labels—floppy disk
- ☐ Markers—black
- ☐ Markers—highlighter
- ☐ Overnight courier forms and envelopes
- ☐ Pads—sticky notes
- ☐ Pads—message
- ☐ Paper clips—standard and jumbo
- ☐ Paper—copier/fax/printer
- ☐ Pencils
- ☐ Pens
- ☐ Printer ink/toner
- ☐ Rubber bands
- ☐ Stamps—self-stick or stamp machine
- ☐ Staples
- ☐ Stationery—letterhead and plain
- ☐ Tape—cellophane
- ☐ Tape—packing

SAMPLE FILE INDEX

IDEAS FOR ORGANIZING FILES

A FILE INDEX IS A ROAD MAP OF YOUR FILING SYSTEM—AND THE BACKBONE OF A WELL-ORGANIZED OFFICE. THE FOLLOWING FILE INDEX (FOR A LOCAL WATER RESOURCES DISTRICT) SHOWS HOW ONE OFFICE ORGANIZES ITS FILES.

ADMINISTRATION

(Drawer #1)

Forms

Insurance

Labor Regulations

Office Lease/Agreement

Operations Handbook

Tax Exemption

Unemployment Claims

BUDGET/FINANCIAL

(Drawer #2)

FY '98 Appropriations

FY '98 Budget

FY '98 Funding

FY '99 Appropriations

FY '99 Budget

FY '99 Funding

Audit

Invoices Paid

Vendors *(filed alphabetically)*

GRANTS

(Drawer #3)

Administration Grant

Forms

Monitoring

Nonpoint Source

Water Quality Management

MEMBERSHIP

(Drawer #4)

Annual Report

Board of Directors—Member Info

Board of Directors—Minutes

Dues

Membership Directory

Mission and Goals Statement

Position Statements

PRESS/PUBLICATIONS

(Drawer #5)

Construction Grants

Federalism

Groundwater

News Releases

PROGRAMS

(Drawer #6)

Clean Water Act Reauthorization

Construction Grants

Enforcement

Groundwater

Monitoring and Standards

Pollution Prevention

Safe Drinking Water Act

State Revolving Loan Fund

Watershed

Wetland

SUCCESSFUL SPEAKING

POINTERS FOR A POLISHED PRESENTATION

———— ✳ ————

GIVING A SPEECH OR MAKING A PRESENTATION NEED NOT BE A HARROWING ORDEAL. BY PREPARING CAREFULLY AND USING THESE WELL-TESTED TECHNIQUES, YOU CAN MAKE YOUR CASE WITH FLAIR.

PREPARING THE TALK

◆ Decide on the goal of your presentation and write down your central theme.

◆ Organize your points logically.

◆ Think of personal anecdotes or humorous stories to engage your audience from the start.

◆ Tailor the speech to the age, gender, and profession of your audience.

◆ Think of rhetorical questions you can ask to get your audience involved.

◆ Use testimony, studies, and statistics to prove your point.

◆ Plan visual aids to supplement your presentation.

◆ Think about questions—especially the difficult ones—your audience is likely to ask, and plan how you'll respond.

◆ Videotape your presentation for review, or practice in front of a coworker who can offer constructive criticism.

GIVING THE TALK

◆ Arrive early to set up everything and to test any equipment you'll be using.

◆ Introduce your topic so the audience knows what to expect.

◆ Make eye contact with members of the audience.

◆ Speak quickly enough that you hold the audience's interest but slowly enough that they can absorb the material.

◆ Stand up straight.

◆ Speak to your audience: Don't read from note cards or visual aids.

◆ Be lively and energetic.

◆ Summarize your points to leave your audience with the key issues.

◆ Allow adequate time in your presentation to answer questions.

◆ If you don't know the answer to a question, promise to find out.

Business Travel Checklist

PACKING LIST FOR BUSINESS TRAVELERS

———————— ✳ ————————

Packing the right items—but not too many—when you travel is vital for a successful business trip. Keep toiletries and other small essentials prepacked in bags so you can simply grab them and go.

ESSENTIALS

- ☐ Tickets
- ☐ Passport and necessary visas
- ☐ Itinerary
- ☐ Address book
- ☐ Car/hotel confirmation numbers
- ☐ Maps and directions
- ☐ Foreign language books
- ☐ Daily planner or calendar
- ☐ Appointment information
- ☐ Calculator
- ☐ Notepad
- ☐ Business cards
- ☐ Medications
- ☐ Basic toiletries and makeup
- ☐ One or more business outfits
- ☐ Reading glasses/contact lenses
- ☐ Cash and credit cards
- ☐ Small bills for tipping

ELECTRONICS

- ☐ Cell phone
- ☐ Cell phone charger or extra battery
- ☐ Pager and spare battery
- ☐ Computer or PDA
- ☐ AC adapter and cables
- ☐ External floppy disk drive, CD-ROM drive, and blank disks
- ☐ Modem and connector cable

- ☐ Phone cord (with RJ-11 connectors)
- ☐ AC extension cord or power strip
- ☐ Electrical and phone adapters

PRESENTATION TOOLS

- ☐ Overhead transparencies or slides
- ☐ Laser pointer
- ☐ Handouts (or master copy)
- ☐ Company brochures
- ☐ Product samples

OFFICE SUPPLIES

- ☐ Notepaper or letterhead
- ☐ Envelopes
- ☐ Blank overnight courier forms
- ☐ Return-address labels
- ☐ Stapler and staples
- ☐ Pens and pencils
- ☐ Sticky notes
- ☐ Several file folders

MISCELLANEOUS

- ☐ Money belt or pouch
- ☐ Portable alarm clock
- ☐ Neck/back pillow
- ☐ Motion sickness wrist bands
- ☐ Luggage tags
- ☐ Earplugs and eye mask
- ☐ Fold-up raincoat or umbrella

DAYTIME CONTACTS

KEY PHONE NUMBERS TO HAVE ON HAND

------------ ✳ ------------

Whether you're at the office or at home for the day, you'll need a list of essential names and numbers. Fill in the contact sheet below and keep a copy by the phone at work and at home.

MEDICAL/DENTAL

Family doctor:_____

Pediatrician:_____

Family dentist:_____

Orthodontist:_____

Insurance:_____

Pharmacy (local):_____

Veterinarian:_____

EMERGENCIES

Poison control:_____

Local fire station:_____

Local police:_____

Pharmacy (24-hour):_____

Alarm company:_____

Taxi service:_____

Neighbor:_____

You'll be glad you have emergency numbers handy.

HOME REPAIR

Electrician:_____

Heat/air:_____

Plumber:_____

Gas company:_____

Other: _____

FOR THE BABYSITTER

Mom's work:_____

Dad's work:_____

Other relative:_____

Pediatrician:_____

IN CASE YOU'RE SICK

Supervisor:_____

Coworkers:_____

_____

Important clients:_____

_____

_____

MISCELLANEOUS

Day care:_____

Babysitter:_____

School(s):_____

_____

_____

Weather report:_____

Traffic information:_____

LAUNCHING A BUSINESS

TIPS FOR STARTING OUT

———— ✴ ————

R UNNING A BUSINESS OUT OF YOUR HOME CAN BE AN APPEALING PROSPECT, BUT YOUR NEW VENTURE WON'T THRIVE UNLESS YOU TAKE A BUSINESSLIKE APPROACH TO PLANNING AND RUNNING IT. HERE ARE SOME POINTERS TO HELP.

PLANNING

◆ Determine whether you can really cope with the demands, isolation, and uncertainties of self-employment.

◆ Talk to everyone you know who has relevant experience.

◆ Evaluate your target market to determine if you can make enough profit.

◆ Figure out if you can support your family during the first few lean years.

◆ Create a business plan, paying special attention to marketing and setting interim goals for productivity, growth, and earnings.

DEVELOPMENT

◆ Network with colleagues and potential clients whenever you can.

◆ Acquire business savvy through workshops, targeted reading, and mentors.

◆ Volunteer with professional organizations to gain recognition.

MANAGEMENT

◆ Keep in touch with positive, optimistic people who believe in you.

◆ Manage your time so that you are doing the tasks that count.

◆ Outsource the aspects of your business that you don't enjoy.

◆ Keep both overhead and expenses low until income justifies expansion.

◆ Practice win-win negotiation skills so that both parties walk away happy.

◆ Learn to present yourself well so that others have confidence in you.

◆ Make sure your place of business makes a positive impression.

◆ Admit when you've made errors, then do all you can to rectify the situation.

◆ Learn from the mistakes of others.

◆ Set limits on how much your business will interfere with your personal life.

RESOURCES

L OOKING FOR ADDITIONAL DETAILS AND GUIDANCE? TURN TO THESE PUBLICATIONS, RETAIL SUPPLIERS, ORGANIZATIONS, AND OTHER RESOURCES—THEY CAN HELP MAKE YOUR WORK LIFE MORE ENJOYABLE AND PRODUCTIVE.

PUBLICATIONS

365 Ways to Simplify Your Work Life: Ideas That Bring More Time, Freedom, and Satisfaction to Daily Work
By Odette Pollar
(Dearborn Financial, 1996)

Cultural Diversity in the Workplace
By Sally J. Walton
(Irwin Professional, 1994)

Dig Your Well Before You're Thirsty: The Only Networking Book You'll Ever Need
By Harvey Mackay
(Doubleday, 1997)

How the Best Get Better
By Dan Sullivan
(800) 387-3206
Audiotape series with booklet.

How to Be #1 With Your Boss: How to Keep Your Job Longer and Enjoy It More
By Don Aslett
(Marsh Creek Press, 1994)

Macworld magazine
(415) 243-0505
http://macworld.zdnet.com
Macintosh computer information.

The On-Purpose Person: Making Your Life Make Sense
By Kevin W. McCarthy
(Navpress, 1992)

PC Magazine
(303) 665-8930
www.zdnet.com/pcmag
High-tech news and reviews.

PC World magazine
(800) 825-7595
www.pcworld.com
PC news and product reviews.

Smart Networking: How to Turn Contacts Into Cash, Clients, and Career Success
By Anne Baber and Lynne Waymon
(Kendall/Hunt, 1997)

Speak Like a Pro: A Business Tool for Marketing and Managing
By Margaret Bedrosian
(BCI Press, 1994)

Stairway to Success: The Complete Blueprint for Personal Success and Professional Achievement
By Nido R. Qubein
(John Wiley & Sons, 1997)

Stick to It! The Power of Positive Persistence
By C. Leslie Charles
(Yes! Press, 1995)

Technotrends
By Daniel Burrus, with Roger Gittines
(HarperBusiness, 1993)

Working Mother magazine
(800) 627-0690
Aimed at women who are raising children while pursuing a career.

Working Solo
By Terri Lonier
(John Wiley & Sons, 1998)

Working Woman magazine
(800) 234-9675
A publication devoted to today's businesswoman.

You Don't Have to Go Home From Work Exhausted! A Program to Bring Joy, Energy, and Balance to Your Life
By Anne McGee-Cooper
(Bantam Doubleday Dell, 1992)

SUPPLIERS
Magellan's Travel Supplies
110 W. Sola Street
Santa Barbara, CA 93101
(800) 962-4943
www.magellans.com
A wide range of products that make travel more comfortable, safe, and rewarding.

MicroWarehouse
(computer products for PC)
MacWarehouse
(computer products for Macintosh)
DataComWarehouse
(networking products)
P.O. Box 3014
Lakewood, NJ 08701
(800) 397-8508
www.warehouse.com
These online sites also feature an extensive selection of accessories and fax and copier supplies.

MobilePlanet
21216 Vanowen Street
Canoga Park, CA 91303
(800) 675-2638
www.mobileplanet.com
*Catalog with mobile technology
solutions, including technological
and travel products.*

Planner Pads
5088 S. 107th Street
Omaha, NE 68127-0187
(402) 592-0676
*Calendar planning system for
categorizing, prioritizing, and
scheduling; mail order only.*

Red Dot Systems
(800) 520-0010
*An ingenious combination of brief-
case and portable filing system for
truly accessible files on the road.*

Reliable Home Office
P.O. Box 1501
Ottawa, IL 61350-9916
(800) 869-6000
*Furniture, electronic equipment,
storage units, and accessories for
the home office.*

ORGANIZATIONS
**Association of Records
Managers and Administrators,
Inc. (ARMA International)**
4200 Somerset Drive, Suite 215
Prairie Village, KS 66208
(800) 422-2769
www.arma.org/hq
*ARMA provides records retention
guidelines for various industries.
Consult its online catalog of professional resources, including books,
tapes, and videos.*

**National Association of
Professional Organizers (NAPO)**
1033 La Posada Drive, Suite 220
Austin, TX 78752-3880
www.napo.net
*Call the association's referral line at
(512) 206-0151 to request a professional organizer in your area.*

**National Federation of Business
and Professional Women's
Clubs, Inc. (BPW/USA)**
www.bpwusa.org
*BPW/USA promotes legislation
and public policy issues of concern
to working women, and provides
a variety of services and training
for its members.*

Small Business Administration
www.sbaonline.sba.gov
*The Web site of the U.S. govern-
ment agency providing information
and services for small businesses.*

**Telephone Preference Service
Direct Marketing Association**
P.O. Box 9014
Farmington, NY 11735-9014
www.the-dma.org
*Send a letter with your name,
address, and phone number to be
removed from telemarketing lists.*

Toastmasters International
www.toastmasters.org
*Toastmasters' clubs provide tools
that enable people to develop effective communication skills.*

**Women's Network for Entre-
preneurial Training (WNET)**
www.sba.gov/womeninbusiness
/wnetcov.html
*Successful entrepreneurs mentor
women whose businesses are a
year old and ready to grow.*

OTHER RESOURCES
3M Post-it Software Notes
www.mmm.com/psnotes
*The electronic version of Post-it
Notes for your computer screen.*

**Fit 10: Your 10-Minute
Exercise Solution**
(888) 726-5954
*A compact, lightweight, and
portable exercise system that
fits in your suitcase.*

Great Ideas software
(919) 220-8177
*Tips program with useful infor-
mation on technology, productivity,
the Internet, and more.*

**Kiplinger's Taming the Paper
Tiger software**
(800) 430-0794
www.thepapertiger.com
*A nonscanning indexing system for
managing paper and other resources.*

Office Ergonomics
www.ur-net.com/office-ergo
*A Web site offering practical
information and advice about
good ergonomic practices.*

Women's Web
www.womweb.com
*A Web site specializing in women's
issues and women in business.*

ZD Net At Home
www.zdnet.com/athome
*Information on computers and
technology in the home office.
Contains a number of useful
links to other Web sites.*

INDEX

ACKNOWLEDGMENTS

ADDITIONAL PHOTOGRAPHY: **FPG** 24 Ron Chapple; 33 Rob Gage. **Philip Harvey** 70. **The Image Bank** 61 Steve Niedorf; 85 Romilly Lockyer; 113 David De Lossy. **Liaison International** 71 Churchill & Klehr; 98 Jim Cummins. **The Stock Market** 15, 55 Jose Pelaez; 119 C/B Productions. **Tony Stone Images** 12 Tim Brown; 21 Richard Shock; 48, 52, 87 Bruce Ayres; 90 Walter Hodges; 109 Charles Thatcher. **Westlight** 36 Ron Watts; 118 Steve Smith. SPECIAL THANKS: The publishers wish to thank the following people for their valuable help during the creation of this book: Desne Border, Rick Clogher, Karl Koessel, and Mimi Lathan Towle for editorial assistance; Ken DellaPenta for indexing. Thanks also to Herman Miller, Inc. (Zeeland, MI), for the loan of photographic props. AUTHORS' ACKNOWLEDGMENTS: Barbara Hemphill and Pam Gibbard wish to thank Odette Pollar for introducing us to Roger Shaw; our clients, who are always wonderful teachers; our NAPO colleagues, who provide constant inspiration—and especially Holly Gershuny, without whom we could never have met our deadlines.